Revelation and Healing

This book is dedicated to my friends and family, teachers, counselors, students (who are also my teachers), co-workers, Compañeros y Compañeras, *Rosa Parks, Rev. Dr. Martin Luther King Jr., John Lewis, Harriet Tubman, Rufina Amaya, Josephine Baker, and Rev. John Baumann, SJ.*

Revelation and Healing

A Father and Son Reunion

Morgan Zo Callahan

Honoring Lionel Durand

1920 Port-au-Prince, Haiti
1961 Paris, France

Morgan Zo Callahan was born in New York City, studied at Jesuit schools, received an MA in Philosophy at Gonzaga University, took courses in political philosophy at Stanford University's Hoover Institute, and trained as a community organizer at the Alinsky Institute in Chicago. For eighteen years he taught mental fitness at convalescent hospitals, where he became interested in hospice work. Currently he teaches adult-school ESL, coaches writing for university students, and also tutors high school and elementary school students. He's been fortunate to have traveled widely, meeting along the way many wonderful, interesting people in Taiwan, South Korea, Mexico, El Salvador, Spain, Morocco, Costa Rica, Canada, Guatemala, Panama, Nicaragua, Honduras, Italy, the Bahamas, and the Dominican Republic. Morgan is the author of *Red Buddhist Envelope, Bamboo Bending,* and the co-author of *Intimate Meanderings: Conversations Close to Our Hearts,* published by iUniverse. He contributed a chapter to *Transitions in the Lives of Jesuits and Former Jesuits* and one to *A Thousand Hands: A Guidebook to Caring for Your Buddhist Community,* published by Sumeru Press. Morgan's articles have appeared in *Karmakaze* and *Common Sense* (Los Angeles Buddhist Union). His poetry was published in anthologies of the Southern California Haiku Study Group: 2013 (*Dandelion Breeze*), 2014 (*Apology of Wild Flowers*), 2016 (*What the Wind Can't Touch*), 2017 (*Eclipse Moon*), and 2020 (*A Sonic Boom of Stars*); *All My Tomorrows,* Volume VI, 1993; *Full Moon Poetry Society,* 2011 and 2012; *Atlas Poetica: A Journey of Poetry of Place in Contemporary Tanka* (Summer 2012); and *Altadena Poetry Review Anthology 2018.*

*I will no longer act on the outside
in a way that contradicts the truth
that I hold deeply on the inside.
I will no longer act as if I were less
than the whole person
I know myself
inwardly to be.*
—Rosa Parks

Table of Contents

Foreword

In the fall of 1959—as I was beginning my second year at Loyola High School, a Jesuit prep school in central Los Angeles—Morgan Callahan arrived as a sophomore transfer student. I don't recall the moment that we met. In fact, our paths didn't cross much at all that year. He was a boarding student, and I walked to school from my home, less than a mile away. We were never in the same homeroom during any of the three years that we were classmates at Loyola, but, starting in our junior year, we worked together for two years on the staff of the *El Camino* school yearbook.

I remember Morgan as a bashful boy, universally well-liked, with a quiet, winning personality. He was good-looking and athletic, and competed in track and cross-country running. He was an avid basketball fan and, by his senior year, he became quite a good player. Morgan had an olive complexion with a rosy undertone. His short black hair was very curly. He was quite tall, but his head seemed habitually bent down a bit, as if it were pulled by an unseen weight. His smile was a quick flash of warmth and light. He had an easy laugh. Who wouldn't like Morgan? He somehow managed to get me, a confirmed geek, onto a basketball court my one and only time, playing with our Japanese-American classmates and their friends at a gym in the Little Tokyo neighborhood of downtown Los Angeles.

I was a bright enough student, but not sufficiently motivated to really apply myself. I preferred TV and comic books to homework. I didn't give much thought to helping people less fortunate than I was, so it's quite surprising that Morgan was able to "shanghai" me to accompany him on many

Saturdays during our final few semesters, to spend time with developmentally challenged students in East Los Angeles. Morgan says that I "volunteered," but his gentle sincerity was irresistible. As long as I have known him, Morgan has been a man concerned with and for others.

After we graduated in June 1962, I had a wonderful year in the nascent Honors Program at Santa Clara University, while Morgan spent his first year as a Jesuit novice. When I entered the novitiate myself in the fall of 1963, Morgan was my "guardian angel," showing me the ropes of religious life. He seemed a little more serious, as novices tend to be, but he was just as quick as ever to smile, and, above all, he was kind. During the next several years, we alternated being together for a year and then apart for a year as we engaged in our undergraduate studies. We both completed our BA degrees at Gonzaga University in 1968, and then spent another year there together in a graduate philosophy program. Morgan was always there for me as a quiet, benevolent presence.

I spent two years in graduate studies while teaching college classes. Meanwhile, Morgan was teaching high school students, with a summer in Chicago learning the ropes of community organizing. By 1972 we were both on our way out of the Jesuits. We met again by serendipity that fall at a small, experimental liberal arts college in northern California where both of us taught for a while, Morgan for two years while I stayed on for sixteen. After those two years together at New College, we didn't see each other for almost a quarter century.

Looking back, I am both amazed and chagrined that we spent almost fifteen years in fairly close contact, often living right down the hall from each other, yet I never really took advantage of the opportunity to get to know Morgan all that well. We always had a warm and friendly relationship, but, due in great part to my own makeup, the connection was not as deep as it could have been. My temperament, which tends to make me more at home in my head than in my heart, was reinforced by the prevailing culture I grew up in, including my Jesuit training that emphasized the intellectual over the emotional. Getting really close to anyone has always been a challenge for me, but—thanks to some good friends like Morgan—I've been doing better lately.

Having retired around the turn of the millennium, I was able to start attending the annual reunions of a group of former Jesuits from the West Coast. Morgan was there most years too. He was more active than ever in numerous projects to serve poor and marginalized people in Mexico and Central America, and in drumming up support for the work of Fr. John Baumann, SJ, facilitating faith-based community organizing in the USA and internationally in Haiti, El Salvador, and Rwanda. Morgan's concern is always with real people, and his work is direct and personal. The people he touches come to realize that he loves them, and he is warmly loved in turn by all of them.

John Suggs is another former Jesuit who has been very active in our group's activities and governance. He has been a wonderful friend to Morgan. Over the course of the past twenty years, John has become a proficient and dedicated professional genetic genealogist, doing research to help adoptees to identify, and in some cases to reunite with, their birth parents and their biological families. He has devoted himself with extraordinary energy to this mission. Just a few years ago I became aware that Morgan had been adopted when he was a toddler, and that he had discovered some basic information about his birth mother while we were still in high school. Thanks to John's great generosity and strong research skills, Morgan learned much more about his mother and her family roots. I was deeply saddened as I felt Morgan's excitement turn to disappointment—and then to hurt—at finding that her family didn't want to have anything to do with him. Knowing what a gentle, good, and giving person Morgan is, the rejection was all the more painful to watch. For the past seven years, John has contributed an enormous amount of his time and employed his skills to help Morgan discover his biological father and his father's extended family, gradually and systematically moving closer and closer to their genetic quarry until the final breakthrough came that this book chronicles and celebrates.

Morgan wrote a short article for *The Haitian Times*, published in August 2019, that related the story of that breakthrough. Based on the positive response to that article, he decided to expand it into a full-length book. I've helped Morgan with editing and publishing two previous books, so when Morgan asked me to help with this new book about his "reunion" with a father he never met, and who never even knew that he had a son, I realized very well what I would be getting myself into. I told Morgan honestly that I was getting too old and decrepit for this kind of effort, and that I wouldn't do it for anyone else in the world. But how could I not say yes? Morgan continues to be irresistible.

After Morgan had written most of the book, another breakthrough occurred that I was able to witness as it unfolded in real time. One of his father's relatives came across the *Haitian Times* article and got in touch with Morgan. One relative reached out to another, until soon the floodgates were open and Morgan was deluged with messages from nephews and cousins who welcomed him joyfully and excitedly into their family. Sharing in this experience was one of the most emotionally moving and rewarding moments of my life.

And so, at long last, I've begun to know Morgan more deeply, and to realize how important he is to me—as he is to so many others. Better late than never.

Robert R. Rahl

Preface

Those who do not have power over the story that dominates their lives, power to retell it, deconstruct it, joke about it, and change it as time changes, truly are powerless because they cannot think new thoughts.
—Salman Rushdie

On August 16, 2019, I was excited that *The Haitian Times* published a three-page story in their online newspaper, "First Person—A Father and Son Reunion," which recounts my discovering that the eminent Haitian journalist and fighter for the French Resistance, Lionel Durand, was my biological father. (See Appendix 1.) A few readers from Haiti, now living in the United States, responded that the article made them proud to have been born in Haiti. "Your story is worthy of a longer article or a book." "Can you write about what it was like for your father as a Black member of the Resistance and how it relates to the Black movement for human and civil rights that has made positive strides but continues today?" "Did you participate in the civil rights movement when you were a young man?" "How can the Diaspora of Haiti stay connected to Mother Haiti and continue to serve from, with, and for the beautiful, long-suffering people?" "Would you tell us more of the stories Lionel Durand wrote?"

Extremely happy about my life-changing discovery, my wife Dori, stepson David, and daughter-in-law Betty enthusiastically urged me to expand my *Haitian Times* article. In Appendix 2, many other encouraging reactions to the article are posted. They motivate me—in the hope that it will benefit others—to share my year-long individual therapy, opening me to a full, joyous acceptance of Lionel Durand as my father and the consequent longing to make his short life more widely known. Some of the personal emails I received from adoptees and others shared stories about the healing of trauma. In a long email, a woman who, after a painful, conflicted search found her biological parents and was in therapy, suggested I write about my psychological process as a child adopted in the late1940s, as she had been. She told me she received extended therapy to help her understand the emotional repercussions of learning a few years ago that, as a newborn baby, she was abandoned and left at a convent door with a note, "Sorry." She wished healing by extension to others to finally cope more peacefully with self-defeating demons of self-hatred and shame, which, without understanding why until therapy, plagued her most of her life. "I have inexplicably—and not without some complications—found myself loving myself as well as others, respecting, and caring for myself, considering my best interests, knowing my boundaries, and taking advantage of available means for healing." I felt so moved by her story and good will towards others that I took her suggestion to heart.

I was asked questions but was not sure I could answer them satisfactorily. "Would you say that there are avenues of help for those wounded by their separation from their biological parents?" "What were the circumstances of your adoption?" "How did you come to feel whole again?" "I feel many are being traumatized by COVID-19." "What about the severe suffering of so many children still being destroyed by child trafficking, wars, and violence?" "Can we truly heal personal trauma in the midst of collective trauma?"

And I had some of my own questions that might motivate me to bite the bullet and write. Could this story be uplifting for Haitians and others? Would someone who was hesitant to do a DNA search be nudged to do it? Would there be someone who reads about my own healing of trauma be animated to work with whatever troublesome trauma, from adoption or not, he or she might be facing? Can we truly learn from and support communities which have suffered trauma? Can we be supportive of the ongoing Black struggles and other people's righteous struggles for social justice and human rights?

Might I be a witness that healing, even if incomplete, can be—paradoxically—a lasting openness to Life? Could I make more widely known the story of my remarkable father, Lionel Durand, a Black man who knew what it was like to be discriminated against up to the end of his life, including under Nazi occupation? Could I pull off this balancing act?

Still reluctant to take on the task of writing a long article or a short book, I had a definitive change of heart after reading online about Faith in Action International Haiti (also in Rwanda and El Salvador) founded by my dear friend, Fr. John Baumann, SJ. (See Appendix 4.) This book is dedicated to him—along with Dr. Martin Luther King Jr., John Lewis, Rufina Amaya, Harriet Tubman, Josephine Baker, and Rosa Parks. Focusing on Haiti was my inertia-breaking inspiration; Lionel's life was too. To the beloved people of Haiti, from our hearts and souls, our small book is sending you positive warm wishes of solidarity.

I met John Baumann in 1970 in Chicago. A mentor for me in the "Saul Alinsky" school of community organizing, he told me to get out there and organize around strongly felt needs in the community, so I've always been aware that the main impetus for change comes, not from being imposed upon, but from an enthusiasm deeply felt by the people who want to improve their lives. The people are the main energy that feed a strong, non-violent activism in the spirit of Dr. King, still relevant today. Leaders are called to wisely and humbly, in a spirit of service to our shared humanity, foster we-the-people's agenda and empowerment. As an ideal, I hold the image of Jesus washing his disciples' feet at the Last Supper or Fr. Gregory Boyle, SJ, washing the Homies' feet at Homeboy Industries in Los Angeles. This is especially challenging in our climate of hyper-polarization where, for example, the Republicans and Democrats commonly will only vote in favor of a bill their party introduces, ignoring the value to the people of the bill itself.

With the assurance of help from my 1962 Loyola High School classmate, Robert R. Rahl, and from DNA expert, John F. Suggs—both cherished friends—I committed to write a response to some of our pressing questions, a conversation about matters close to our hearts. So here is our book of revelation and healing, offered with respect, appreciation, and wishes for peace within each of us and in our global neighborhood.

Morgan Zo Callahan

Acknowledgments

Gratitude bestows reverence, allowing us to encounter everyday epiphanies, those transcendent moments of awe that change forever how we experience life and the world.
—John Milton

Appreciation is a wonderful thing. It makes what is excellent in others belong to us as well.
—Voltaire

Don't pray when it rains if you don't pray when the sun shines.
—Leroy Satchel Paige

Thank you, esteemed reader, for your interest. My debt of gratitude starts with you and extends to family, friends, teachers, and students.

There are two treasured *brothers* in particular who made this book possible: John F. Suggs—whom you will hear from and learn about in this book—who wrote the Afterword; and Robert R. Rahl, author of the Foreword, whose guidance, editing, and technical skills unified my writing into a presentable, hopefully enjoyable, whole. Their kindness and patience can never be repaid but they know they are loved, sun shining in my life. My gratitude to Don Maloney for kindly writing the Introduction and for providing valuable editorial advice. Thanks also go to Robert's son, Jeremy Rahl, for designing the cover for this book.

Though I never met them, I want to thank Nancy Verrier and Peter Levine for their books and YouTube videos. Much appreciation wells in my heart for my gifted therapist for a transforming year of therapy.

Merci beaucoup, my Haitian cousins and two nephews, for lovingly connecting me to my newly discovered paternal ancestry. Lionel Durand's painting of his daughter Barbara on the front cover and the Picasso drawing on the back cover are from Lionel Changeur. The photos of Lionel Durand and of Barbara with her father are from Jérémy Changeur. And thank you, Lionel Durand, for being my father, for my DNA, for letting me know you from your heroic, artistic, literary, more-than-full life. I hope this book does you justice and reflects the *joie de vivre*, values, and spirit you generously convey.

Introduction

". . . to carry grief in one hand and gratitude in the other and be stretched large by them."
—Francis Weller

Not just a tale of pain, although there is pain, nor one of easy resolution, although there is eventual closure, this book recounts the author's slow journey from an adoption that left him longing for his biological mother and wondering about his biological father. Discovering, while in high school, his mother's identity, years later he found that of his biological father, Lionel Durand, a Black man born in Port-au-Prince, Haiti. Suddenly the author realized the source of his own immediate empathy with Martin Luther King Jr. and the civil rights movement he led.

Recovering painfully from his years of estrangement and loss, the author shares the often-shocking details of his adoption, and the therapies that brought him healing, therapies helpful not only to adoptees but to all who need healing from emotional suffering and losses of all kinds. With a heart "stretched large" by his own experience, the author has traveled to El Salvador and Mexico to accompany the many there who are suffering from collective trauma, poverty and discrimination, victims of systemic injustice, wounded yet unbowed.

Finally, with filial admiration, the author traces the life of his beloved father, Lionel Durand, an internationally acclaimed newsman and journalist, who fought in the French Resistance during World War II, and whose struggles for peace and justice mirror those of our own day.

Welcome to this reading journey and its wondrous surprises.

Dr. G. Donald Maloney
Xavier University
Cincinnati, Ohio

1

From Haunting to Homecoming

We are often haunted by important relationships from the past that influence us unconsciously in the present. As we work them through, they go from haunting to becoming singularly part of our history.
—Norman Doidge

What impelled me to first seek my biological mother and then, late in life as this account reveals, my father?

When my adoption was finalized in 1949 (5 years old), I was living 48 miles from New York City in Norwalk, Connecticut, with my adoptive parents, whom I sincerely and uniquely revere/love as much as I specially and naturally love my biological mother and father. Our blood matters, our DNAs are our unique blueprints of physical and psychological traits and growth, inviolable treasures even when diamonds in the rough. Regrets and heartache, even traumas, yes, there are some among abundant blessings of healing and feeling connected.

From my earliest years, I often desired to reunite with my biological mother. Where's Mother? Even in her absence, she was tangibly with me as a mysterious, tender, protective presence. My first home was Mother's warm, nourishing womb. Thank you, Mother, for carrying and birthing me, you carry no debts to me. On certain occasions, fantasies of intimate reunion would overtake my consciousness and feelings. I would see a movie in my mind: *being welcomed back, hugged, and kissed tenderly by Mother.*

As a little boy, I would walk down the road to, in my mind, go back to my original home; my adoptive parents would ask where I was going, and assure me I was now in my new house with my own large bedroom upstairs. Soon I adapted. As I got older, I would ask my parents about my mother and *why am I dark?* I was told I was probably French, as French was all I spoke when I first arrived at my new home. My adoptive family only spoke English. I pressed more about my race, but my parents were evasive and uncomfortable so this desire *to know my origins* had to be mostly hidden. Within, I determinedly vowed to continue the search.

I was relatively happy living with my adoptive family, mother Helen, father Morgan Sr., and sister Mary, also adopted. Recently I received an unexpected phone call from Mary's only child, Alexandra (name changed for privacy), who was born out of wedlock in 1967 and adopted when one week old. About 10 years ago, she hired an agency which found that Mary was her biological mother. Alexandra reached out to Mary, but Mary (who never had the desire to know her biological daughter) did not want to reconnect. Alexandra understood Mary's wish not to revisit the past, but still wanted to find out about her biological mom, at least have a picture of Mary. She said she was curious to know more about Mary's life and personality. We had long phone conversations about Mary, and I was able to answer some of Alexandra's questions about Mary's life. To Alexandra's delight, I sent her not only photos of Mary but also a picture of Alexandra when she was a newborn baby.

Living close to nature in the country, sports-crazy, going to NYC with my father, walking in the buzzing, magical City and taking refreshing cool-down swims in the Atlantic Ocean, there was a vibrancy to my life. I looked forward to catching grounders from my father on the freshly mowed grass and to listening to the stories and reflections of Catholic theology of my mother on rainy or snowed-in afternoons.

My dad was often given tickets to see Mickey Mantle's magnificent Bronx Bombers. I listened, always alone, to their games on the radio broadcast by exuberant sportscaster Mel Allen (1913-1996). I rooted fanatically for the New York Yankees; occasionally I would angrily throw my radio across the room when they lost. Yankee Stadium was my favorite cathedral (more than St. Patrick's), a source of awe and wonder, pungent smells of excessive mustard on my hot dog and the freshly manicured so-green grass and rosy-brown dirt playing-field, sounds of rallying music, cheering and booing, feeding on crowd energy, the unexpected showering of life and excitement that gathered all my youthful enthused attention. I saw the majestic Say Hey Kid, the NY Giants' spectacular, graceful Willie Mays (1931-2017) in the Polo Grounds. Our hats are off to honor Willie, an American masterpiece. February 13, 2017: "The great center fielder, whose cap flew off every time he ran the bases, was cut down by a heart attack."

A great hero of my youth was the gallant and dignified, yet tough, Jackie Robinson (1919-1972), and—in awe—I visited Ebbets Field to see him play with the Dodgers. My abiding memory of him is his stealing and sliding across home plate in the 1955 World Series, with Yankees catcher Yogi Berra going crazy. Dem Bums—to my dismay—finally won! Jackie's plea was for an end to discrimination and police brutality against Black people, a brutality he experienced himself in 1971 as he tried one afternoon to enter Harlem's majestic Apollo Theater to visit with friends. "On my way into the lobby, an officer, a plain clothesman, accosted me. He asked me roughly where I was going, and I asked what the hell business it was of his. He grabbed me and spectators passing by told me later that he had pulled out his gun. I was so angry at his grabbing me and so busy telling him he'd better get his hands off me that I didn't remember seeing a gun. By this time people had started crowding around, excitedly telling him my name, and he backed off." (Michael G. Long, "Honor Jackie Robinson, Activist," *Los Angeles Times,* August 23, 2020)

In 2020, it was seventy-three years since Jackie courageously started playing ball professionally, breaking the "color barrier," despite enduring vicious racist taunting and facing segregated hotels, restaurants, transportation, and water fountains. In the book, *First Class Citizenship: The Civil Rights Letters of Jackie Robinson* (Times Books, 2007, edited by Michael G. Long), I read Jackie's letter to President Kennedy after the 1963 assassination of Medgar Evers. "Utilize every federal facility to protect a man (Dr. Martin Luther King Jr.) sorely needed for this era." Medgar Evers (World War II veteran, 38-year-old NCAAP secretary of Jackson, Mississippi) was a civil rights activist who was murdered, shot in the back in the driveway of his Jackson home on June 12, 1963 by KKK member and White supremacist, Byron De La Beckwith. Evers had organized boycotts, calls for strong "economic pinches," against businesses that discriminated against Black people. Dr. King organized a march in protest. After the first two trials of De La Beckwith ended in hung juries, it would not be until 1994 that De La Beckwith would be found guilty of Medgar's murder.

As a young boy, who did not have close friends until high school, I discovered older adults to be good company, fascinating, honest, wise, no-nonsense, sometimes gruff and grouchy, yet encouraging, somewhat mysterious. When not playing sports, roaming in nature, or in school, I was eager to be in their company. In grammar school, I visited older neighbors who did not seem to have younger people around them but were welcoming to me. One day I was walking past a large, but run-down home where Mrs. Davenport was pruning bushes in her front yard. She lived alone and seemed to be a recluse. She had the reputation of being a shrew, and instilled fear in the kids who sometimes played pranks on her. On this particular occasion, she asked me if I would help her by putting tree branches into a wheelbarrow and moving them, which I did, while casting a suspicious eye on her, remembering some of the other kids had said that she was a bona fide witch who kept her rifle next to the front porch door. Apart from her unsmiling wizened face, I found nothing sinister about her. Her comments on plants, flowers, trees, squirrels, rabbits, muskrats, dogs, and cats mesmerized me. She never spoke about other people except saying that a group of "lousy boys" had thrown rocks at her dogs. After I finished giving her a hand, she invited me to enjoy freshly baked chocolate-chip cookies and cool, rich milk. That treat and conversation began our friendship. I looked forward to visiting her, walking down the long driveway, knocking on her door, doing some short chore, then letting chocolate melt in my mouth, drinking cold milk, gaining entrance into magical conversations. I looked at her photo albums, seeing her as a pretty young woman with an engaging smile; I inspected her "favorite contraptions." Once I opened a painted music box, inlaid with white-spotted black and orange butterflies—the box released a melody that brought such delight to Mrs. Davenport, her face noticeably softened.

Until my knees gave out, my favorite activity was to play basketball. I discovered "in-the-zone" competition and camaraderie playing at the public parks, indoor gyms, and at the beach. That is irreplaceable: playing hoops. Rich memories remain and inform my present-day sensibilities, which go beyond the great game itself, leading to an appreciation of the NBA's long history of support for the ideals of Dr. Martin Luther King Jr. I started playing basketball in 1957, a bench-warmer for Jackson Sunoco, Norwalk's Biddy League 1957–1958 champs. I found practicing to be exhilarating even though embarrassing for my lack of skill. I would not develop into a decent basketball player until my senior year in high school when I started to go more frequently to public venues for pickup games. Just as basketball was a passion for me from boyhood to maturity, so too from youth up to this day, as a venerable senior, I have connected with the NBA players who helped raise my consciousness about non-violent protests against racism (towards anyone) and for inclusion, justice, equality, and brother-sisterhood. NBA players have had for many years a unique and far-reaching platform to rally for change that promotes the common good, wishing well, wishing love and peace for all, as best we can, bruised but not broken, human beings.

****

I am very fond of and grateful for my adoptive cousins (and their families) who were more free-flowing than my Callahan family: Rod, Annie, Bimmie, and Bruce. May Bruce Enjoy Eternal Ease and Happiness. These sweet people have enriched my life since boyhood through play, family gatherings, support in hard times, catching up conversations, laughter, tears, stories, growing up in our unique ways, connecting, drifting apart, and reconnecting.

As a child, I was conflicted at times, secretive, frustrated, and lonely; I would release tension by chewing the ends of rugs when alone in the living room. On many nights I would go to sleep soothed by candy dissolving in my mouth, later producing many cavities, a substitute compulsively craved sweetness and warmth. Being separated from my biological mother manifested as a tight knot in my stomach and caved in posture. My adoptive father was often gone on business trips; he called me "Black Irishman," which family members thought to be humorous, but was unsettling to me. Schoolmates would tell me: "You don't look like your blond sister, why do you have curly hair?" Painfully self-conscious, I would disappear outside in nature, climb trees for hours, look for animals in the woods, go fishing at a pristine lake, lie down in open fields, self-transcended to other worlds. I sometimes was oblivious to the time and came home after dinnertime. Consequently, I might be "grounded" or receive a strong spanking on my buttocks from my father who used the back of a large, long-handled silver brush.

My parents hired a young lady to help take care of Mary and me. I remember her giving me baths and even in the hot water, I sat cold in an inner retreat, not wanting to be touched. Later, in happy contrast, I came to know an occasional second nanny, French-speaking Louisette, who was warm, affectionate, and attentive. Her French-accented, melodic English relaxed my usual guardedness, bringing me contentment and joy, opening my heart. Sometimes I would daydream that Louisette was really *my mother,* who would come from time to time to be with me. I was helped to heal by Louisette. I remember emotionally to this day one time, when I was grounded, going to her as she was relaxing on the sofa. Nobody was home but Louisette and me. I lay my head on her lap, as if falling into a well of soothing crystal waters. Louisette knew I was being punished but she didn't communicate any judgment of me. After some moments of silence, Louisette tenderly ran her hands through my hair. "You are a lovely delightful sweet boy with dark soft curly hair, and I love you so much. And I always will." Being grounded didn't hurt so much after that.

My father commuted daily to NYC, working successfully as an attorney for the American Can Company and then for Remington (my father had dozens of Remington electric shavers, which I liked to play with). My father decided to go for his dream of having a private practice, so in 1957 he rented an office, hired a secretary, and put out his sign in downtown Norwalk, Connecticut. Unfortunately, few well-paying clients showed up during his two-year private practice. I remember one gentleman, who said he lost money in the stock market, paid my father with a striking ceramic painting from Russia. Dad would come home, desolate and withdrawn. Even my parents' nightly pre-dinner martinis turned from a lively, enjoyable occasion into arguments about money. "Art doesn't pay bills." My mom, a former fashion stylist, organized fashion shows, including on television, for *McCall*'s magazine. She showed me one brochure that she saved of doing a TV show in Connecticut where there was a fashion show and a question-and-answer session with Mom with last-minute fashion tips and new sewing hints. "Here's your chance to consult a fashion authority on fabrics, fashions, colors, and silhouettes. Avail yourself of her wise clothes counsel—then use her bright ideas in the wardrobe you make for yourself with McCall Printed Patterns to make your sewing easy." After marrying, my mother stayed home and was an admirable homemaker as well as an engaging conversationalist. But at this time, she was angry with my father and would not refrain from berating him.

One dinner, my mom lit into my dad for leaving lucrative jobs in NYC. My dad exploded, smashing his plate with his knife. One shattered piece hit me in the cheek, luckily missing my eye. My mom, sister, and I froze in shock. Seeing blood running down my cheek, my father apologized profusely and later, after talking to my mom, said to me: "Let's drive to Los Angeles, just you and me, and start our new life. I have to begin anew." My mother and sister would join us after my father passed his California Bar Examination. I was working as a caddy that summer at a nearby golf club and told my dad he could have my money. Laughing, he told me not to worry. So, in late August 1959, we got in our car and headed to Los Angeles. I would miss my mom and sister and best friend. In the fall of 1958 just entering freshman year in high school, I wrote in my notebook: "I have my first true friend. I am myself with him and don't feel at all different. His name is Bill Miller." I recently called Bill (the last time I saw him was in 1966) and discovered that he had participated with Dr. King in protests for human rights and responsibilities.

On September 1, 1959 we arrived at Loyola High School of Los Angeles on 1901 Venice Blvd., first going the wrong direction—ending up at the ocean—eventually turning around, and finally arriving at Loyola's campus. We were met by a cordial Fr. Joe Barry, SJ, who told us they had an opening for a working boarder. If I served in the kitchen and dining room of the Jesuits, I would be given tuition and room & board. Boarders were to arrive and get settled no later than Labor Day weekend. My dad helped me with my two suitcases, and Father Barry showed us my new home. We were introduced to a few of the amiable boarders who had already arrived. I emotionally said good-bye to Dad and started my sophomore year adventure a week later, the day after Labor Day, September 8, 1959. My dad rented an inexpensive, small downtown bachelor studio with a Murphy bed. I visited him a few times, but he was depressed and wanted to be alone to study for the California Bar Examination. I have on my wall, with admiration, Morgan Callahan's original California law license, duly admitted and qualified as an Attorney at Law, issued July 30, 1962. My father was ecstatic when, in 1964, he was hired by the law firm of O'Melveny and Myers and, to add frosting to his cake, Dad was hired as an associate professor of Real Estate Law at USC. You made it, Dad! Regrettably, in 1967 he died of metastatic lung cancer at age 61, a disease which also took the life of my mom at age 81. May they Enjoy Eternal Life!

At Loyola I became fond of my Jesuit professors, even thinking someday I'd like to be a teacher like that, and I made friends with several classmates. In the summers of 1960 and 1961, I caddied at Hillcrest Country Club on 10000 W. Pico Blvd. where I would see Jack Benny, Groucho Marx, Danny Kaye, and George Burns, among others, attempt to play the exasperating game of golf. Once in overwhelming frustration, a player flung (with appropriate expletives) all his golf clubs one by one far into the water.

****

While still in high school, I paid a private investigator, who was able somehow to find the name of my biological mother. I wrote to her through the Connecticut State Department of Social Services, whose address was given to me by the detective. She never responded. Over fifty years later, John Suggs would tell me that they never would have forwarded these letters to my mother. All my life I had wondered if she got my letters and chose not to respond. I finally understood and accepted that she had never received them. For the most part, I have never felt any ill will towards my mother whom

I sincerely honor, am uplifted by, and feel compassion for, our relationship always already secure. Through the release of my adoption papers a few months after October 3, 2004, when my biological mother died (May she Eternally Be in the Light, Presence, and Joy of God), and thanks to the magic of the Internet, DNA databases, and expert assistance, I was able to learn more about my biological mother and feel her spirit, empathize, understand, express profound gratitude to her for my life, praise her accomplishments, and admit disappointment that she didn't assure that I would know, by hook or by crook, who my biological father was.

I revere your relationship, mother and father; biologically, spiritually we are united in love. I am forever indebted to you for my life, my genetic rebirth, egg and seed united springing a baby human being, me!

2

My Haitian Father,
My African Ancestry

People will not look forward to posterity who never look backward to their ancestors.
—Edmund Burke

The bus was among the first ways I realized there was a Black world and a White world. . . . People always say that I didn't give up my seat because I was tired, but that isn't true. I was not tired physically. . . . No, the only tired I was, was tired of giving in. . . . I knew someone had to take the first step, and I made up my mind not to move. . . . I would like to be remembered as a person who wanted to be free so other people would also be free.
—Rosa Parks

My 74th year delivered a transformational surprise. With the mighty help of a greatly admired friend, John F. Suggs, I discovered that the eminent Haitian journalist, Lionel Durand, was my father. John specializes in analyzing a person's DNA to help identify, locate, and, ultimately reunite adult adoptees and other persons of unknown parental origins with members of their birth families. As John often reminds us: "DNA doesn't lie." Lionel Durand, wow! I am overwhelmed with gratitude. With spunk and patience, John facilitated my being rooted consciously in my paternal flesh, blood, and spirit. Here is the account of how we found my biological father, Lionel Durand, and how it took a good while to do so.

I had known John for years from the regular reunions, retreats for renewal, in which a group of us former and current Jesuits—*Compañeros*—gathered every year on the gorgeous blue-white-sea-waving-spectacular-splashing shores of Santa Cruz, California. But it was only back in 2014, as I helped edit a collection of essays from our group into a book, *Transitions in the Lives of Jesuits and Former Jesuits,* that I discovered John was working as an investigative genetic genealogist and might help me find my father. Intrigued, I put down John's essay and reached out to talk with him about my situation. I still remember that first phone conversation—the two of us, already bonded by our shared lived experiences as Jesuits, immediately connected on an even deeper level, and we took off on a journey to find my father. It would end up taking us years, meandering down many different paths and all too often hitting dead ends. But together, and with newfound friends and supporters that we encountered along the way, we persisted.

John's and my discovery may sound like a lucky miracle. But it was the result of painstaking work. My DNA test results, measured in aptly named centimorgans (cM), were, unfortunately, all exceedingly small. The results only connected me with matches of people who were quite distantly related to me, and with whom I typically shared a Most Recent Common Ancestor (MRCA) going back seven or eight generations or longer. Clearly too far removed in time and space to successfully work our way down to my father. But John was able to see a telling thread in the test results as the DNA clearly showed that my father's heritage was from sub-Saharan Africa. The DNA test results constituted the first irrefutable proof I had that, yes, I was of mixed race. My father was Black. Because all my distant matches that were coming up were primarily from Haiti, we knew that my father was most likely Haitian. Yet since so few Haitians have tested their DNA in these United States DNA databases, it was unknown how long it would take for a blood relative who was a close enough match to be discovered. John did what he could building out the family trees of the distant matches that we had. I reached out to several of the matches but did not get very far with them when I did. Most of the people were afraid and thought this was some sort of a scam. Several put out the word to their extended families not to speak to me if I would call. I was left wondering. Who was my father? How did he die? Had he even known he was going to be a father? Since I was born in 1944, was he a soldier? Did he die in the War? Was his death the reason I was put up for adoption?

Through the Ancestry.com website, John found a third or fourth cousin, calling her and inquiring about my lineage. She did not have many clues, but said she would be glad to speak with me, but to keep it secret from other disapproving members of the family. John had asked and received her permission to record their phone call so I could hear her voice. I was enchanted by her sweet French accent and calm welcoming me to converse. We talked six times, and I viewed her marvelous art on Facebook. She was full of laughter and good stories, ending each call (but the last) with "Ring, call again soon, *Mon Cheri.*" She told me what it was like to live in Haiti, how it was sometimes hard to be a woman, and about her family and the old days, good and bad. From her I learned that Haitians greatly esteem their children, and it was all but unheard of at the time of my birth to put a baby up for adoption. Even if the parents were not married, someone in the family would take them in. So, part of the shock and reluctance of many we contacted to help me find my

biological father stemmed from cultural shame that I was allowed to be adopted. I had been relinquished and given
away! That was the stigma, not placed on me, the child, but
rather on my birth parents and their extended family for allowing it to have happened in the first place. Unfortunately,
Alzheimer's dimmed my new friend and relative's ability to
converse, so we said good-bye, blessing each other forever.
She was the first person of my blood with whom I had spoken since I was three years old.

On another occasion, John and I met in Miami with an
affable, kind family who flew in from France. Their father's
photo looked so much like me and the name/timelines
seemed to fit, so we asked if they would give John a DNA
sample, which would have been impossible for legal reasons
to do in France. They agreed but the DNA test showed there
was no match. Before that, John found the daughter of my
biological mother's former husband. She kindly provided a
DNA sample showing that her father was not my biological
father. We went back to the drawing board.

Years after John started helping me, he discovered a new
match, this time a second cousin on my father's side. With
such a close match he could finally build out the trees and,
by comparing the DNA with the family information, finally
figure out who my father was! John recounted for me the
happy-ending story of his masterful DNA detective work.

"Today (January 5, 2020) we celebrate the Feast of the
Epiphany. One year ago, I got up very early, while it was still
dark, put on a suit and tie (so as to look respectable and not
scare your second cousin, Simone) and drove to her house
in the city. The afternoon before, I had unsuccessfully cold-
called Simone at her home, and attempted to tell her about
you and how you were adopted as a little boy, and that you

never knew your father until the DNA results revealed that you were Haitian and her second cousin. Confused, Simone passed the phone over to one of her daughters, Pascale, whose family she lived with. Pascale got on the phone, listened respectfully for a few minutes before, assuming I was some sort of a con artist, politely, yet firmly, told me that they were not interested and hung up. Thus, I made my decision to go to their home early the next day and attempt to talk to Simone in person. Preferably while her daughter was still in bed asleep. Armed with pictures of you as a boy and your DNA test results, I knocked on her door. And praise God, Simone opened the door while everyone in the house was still sleeping. Hearing my pleas and seeing your pictures as a boy and the family resemblance, she gave me the names of her grandparents and the contact information of her other son-in law, Eduard, the family's historian. Eduard is the husband of her second daughter, Martine. 'But promise me you will not contact him until late this afternoon as he was up all night and needs his sleep.'"

Morgan looks like members of our family.

"True to my word and stopping only to go to Mass, and to beseech the heavens for assistance, I reviewed the names of all four of Simone's grandparents and worked on the family tree in my car, camping out in front of Martine's house— waiting. Finally, Martine and Eduard emerged with their son in the late afternoon, and we at last made contact! They were so incredibly nice and kind to me, sharing with me more genealogical information that finally, finally, led us, in a little more than a week, to discovering Lionel Durand was your Dad! After all these years of searching he was finally found! You, Morgan, were home! It truly was the Feast of the Epiphany."

John deciphered the bloodlines that ended my search for my biological father. Simone, my newfound biological second cousin, was the granddaughter of Lamercie Durand (1873–1945), who was my father's aunt. By discovering all the siblings of Simone's grandmother Lamercie, one of them would be my grandparent.

At 6:55 a.m., January 15, 2019, auspiciously Dr. Martin Luther King Jr. Day—as if Dr. King were giving me a gift— John Suggs texted: "MORGAN CALL ME. Very important!! We found ur Dad!!!"

****

On the government records of my birth and adoption, it declares "Father Deceased" or "Unknown." My adoption papers state that my "actual" father had died before I was born. I would later learn the records were falsified. Lionel Durand was denied his right to be named as my father on legal documents. I am quite certain my biological mother never told Lionel that she had given birth to his son. My adoption was an illegal one, full of secrecy, an original sin.

"The boy, to be known as Morgan Callahan Jr., is a dark-complexioned child, thin and wiry with curly brown hair and large somewhat solemn eyes. Adopting parents see no need for or value in a psychometric examination of this child and therefore, none is being planned. However, Mrs. Callahan did indicate vague interest in such an examination at 'some future date.' On 11-19-47, on the day before his third birthday, the child for adoption was brought to the house of Mr. and Mrs. Callahan. Nothing is known of this child's life up to this date."

"Nothing is known of this child's life up to this date" struck a chord of buried sadness in my heart for the loss of my three beginning years of existence.

If anyone was in need of a psychometric examination and therapeutic intervention, it was me, a traumatized little boy. But, remarkably, in 2019 I received a psychometric examination with a recommendation for one year of somatic therapy to heal trauma associated with adoption. I wonder if my life would have been different if I had talked so many years ago as a child to a French-speaking therapist.

****

Looking back, I was complimented from time to time for "a cool Afro" and experienced occasional racial taunts. One incident I can play back like a vivid movie in my mind. Fourteen years old and excited to have passed my entrance exams to start my freshman year at Fairfield Preparatory School, I boarded the train to the Jesuit campus. Unknown to me, some of the upper classmen forced freshmen to carry their books. Outraged at seeing this ritual of power-subservience, I was in a high-alert stance when an upperclassman belligerently approached me. "Hey, Boy, carry my books!" snickered the student. Encouraged by his buddies, the upperclassman shoved his books into my chest. Defiant, I defended myself, scattering the books up the train cabin aisle. I received some punches and kicks but was all right and unrepentant. Order was restored. Later that day I was called into the principal's office to be told that I was no longer allowed to commute by train to Fairfield College Preparatory.

Throughout my youth, it never occurred to me that I had Black African blood, but as a boy I was very attracted to a monumental Black Cause, the remarkable Human Cause of

Rev. Dr. Martin Luther King Jr. (1929–1968). Feeling the urgency and holiness of his message, I viewed him, the man I most admired, through starstruck, enthusiastic eyes.

We were invited to write letters in support of the peaceful civil rights movement, a righteous effort which absolutely captivated the attention of a few of my grammarschool teachers, progressive Catholic nuns, Sisters of Mercy, who gave me books and articles by and about Dr. King to read. It was the year—from December 1955 to December 1956—of the Montgomery, Alabama, bus boycott. Dr. Martin Luther King Jr's organization solicited letters of support from many churches, including St. Mary's, our church. The nuns asked students to write letters, not demanding, but inviting, welcoming those who really believed in this action meant to support the brilliant and courageous Dr. King. Stirring words for peaceful activism resonated from his voice and heart like urgent waterfalls of flowers. The nuns did not impose their activism on others yet some of us jumped at the chance to participate and help our hero in a small way. Dr. King's short *The Measure of a Man* (1959) continued to foster a flame in me to be an advocate, in my small but determined way, for social justice and human rights: "The ultimate measure of man is not where he stands in moments of comfort and convenience, but where he stands at times of challenge and controversy." Dr. King wrote and preached "What is Man?" and "The Dimensions of a Complete Life" in the summer of 1958 at Purdue University, which were published by Christian Education Press as *The Measure of a Man*. Loud and necessary, the message came to me as an early adolescent that man is both a biological and a spiritual being, with a challenge for all of us to enlighten our moral social conscience, in our collective lives to face, heal, and end segregation and discrimination.

MLK Jr.'s *Stride Toward Freedom: The Montgomery Story* (1958) educated me about the righteous and successful Montgomery bus boycott, "chronicle of 50,000 Negroes who took to heart the principles of nonviolence (seeking to win an opponent for friendship, rather than to humiliate or defeat him) who learned to fight for their rights with the weapon of love, and who in the process acquired a new estimate of their own human worth." December 1, 1955, Rosa Parks (1913–2005), esteemed and celebrated now, was sitting in the first row of the bus's Black section. The bus driver asked her to give up her seat to a White man. Refusing, "tired of giving in," Rosa told the bus driver "I don't think I should have to stand up." She was taken to jail. African Americans, 40,000 commuters strong, were asked to stay off city buses on December 5, 1955, the day of Rosa's trial. Rosa was found guilty of breaking a city ordinance, ordered to pay a $10 fine and $4 in court fees. The valiant Rosa Parks inspired a 381-day boycott until the Supreme Court established that segregation on buses was unconstitutional on November 13, 1956.

Rosa Parks and her fellow leaders of the Montgomery Bus Boycott (MBB) wisely and successfully depicted her to the press and to the world as a simple, tired, church-going seamstress who was just trying to return home from an honest day's work when she was arrested. That non-threatening image resonated deeply across the nation. Although true, it did not begin to adequately describe who Rosa Parks really was. For Rosa Parks had already spent decades working in the civil rights struggle in the South.

As a young woman, fully twenty-four years before the MBB, Rosa Parks played a leading role in Montgomery's Black community in its defense efforts of the infamous 1931 Scottsboro case. Nine young Black boys, none older than twenty, stood wrongly accused of rape. Holding secret meetings in her home, she and her husband and other local leaders worked to raise money for their defense and plotted ways to save them from being killed. Because of the real risk of the defenders being killed as well, an armed lookout was always posted outside her home when these secret meetings were held. Twenty years later, in 1950, the last of the nine walked out of jail free. (*At the Dark End of the Street: Black Women, Rape, and Resistance—A New History of the Civil Rights Movement from Rosa Parks to the Rise of Black Power* by Danielle L. McGuire, 2010)

In the 1940s, she and her husband hosted Montgomery Voters League meetings in their home, where they encouraged their friends and neighbors to register to vote. Rosa joined the Montgomery NAACP in 1943 and immediately got voted its Branch Secretary. In that capacity she would spend over a decade traveling the backroads of Alabama, and documenting incidents of rapes, killings, and other civil rights abuses. No one knew better than she what the true conditions were like "on the ground."

It was in her role as the Montgomery NAACP Secretary that she was sent to a two-week community organizing training workshop in the Highlander Folk School in Tennessee in the summer of 1955. Highlander was the only desegregated facility in the entire South. It was there that Martin Luther King Jr. first heard in 1957 the song "We Shall Overcome," which would become the anthem of the civil rights movement.

For the rest of her life, she would acknowledge how important and transforming those two weeks at the Highlander Folk School were for her personally. They changed her life and she, in turn, changed the world.

Established in 1932 as a grassroots interracial leadership training school for adults by Myles Horton (1905–1990), Highlander originally held workshops to help local people working for social change develop leadership skills. Later it expanded its efforts to concentrate on labor and anti-poverty organizing. In the early 1950s it changed yet again with a focus on civil rights.

When Rosa left to go to Highlander, she described herself as feeling "rather tense and maybe somewhat bitter over the struggle that we were in." She matter-of-factly said that she was "willing to face whatever came, not because I felt that I was going to be benefitted or helped personally, but because I felt that I had been destroyed too long ago." Her long years of working in the movement, documenting the rapes, murders, and other abuses in rural Alabama, had taken its toll on her.

Her husband refused to go with her and was very upset that she was going. She had to take two weeks off without pay as an assistant tailor at Montgomery Fair. This represented a significant financial sacrifice to her family.

The 48 attendees at the workshop were equally divided, half of them White and half of them Black. Together they would spend the next 14 days living, eating, sharing and discussing the unique problems facing their communities. They pondered how their problems were part of the larger, global human rights movement, and—this was crucial— what concrete steps they could take to change things locally.

Rosa described her experience in this way: "I was 42 years old, and it was one of the few times in my life up to that point when I did not feel any hostility from White people. . . . I felt I could express myself honestly without any

repercussions or antagonistic attitudes from other people. . . . It was hard to leave."

On the last day, as was the practice at Highlander, the
group went around the room individually answering the
question "What concrete things do you plan to do when you
get home?" When it came time for Rosa to speak, she reminded everybody that "I live in Montgomery, which is the
cradle of the Confederacy." She noted that, sadly, "nothing
would happen there because blacks wouldn't stick together."
She said that she held out little hope of any real change coming out of Montgomery. But even as she spoke those disappointing words, in the very way she spoke, candidly and
honestly, something had already changed. She herself had
changed. Those two weeks spent living, working, and eating
in an engaged, desegregated community after a lifetime
spent staring into the abyss that is the brutality of White su-
premacy, had changed her. It was not an accident that barely
five months later she found the courage and self-respect
from within to say "No" when she was told to get to the back
seat of the bus. (*The Rebellious Life of Mrs. Rosa Parks* by
Jeanne Theoharis, 2012)

****

I read about the Little Rock integration crisis. It was given a
lot of press. I became more aware of the depth of racial hatred in my country, but also found some significant good-
heartedness and efficient community-organizing for civil
rights by both Blacks and Whites. I was hopeful that Dr.
King's bravery would initiate meaningful social change. I
continued writing letters in support of Dr. Martin Luther
King Jr.'s captivating work and stirring preaching. Within
the White student society of Little Rock Central High, there
was some overt acceptance of the Black students, as well as

many acts of harassment. Some White students offered active support, but there seemed always to be racial taunting going on. I felt that aligning myself with the positive energy for African-American rights through writing letters was allowing me to dive a little more deeply into this monumental happening for change. I felt drawn as if in an inescapable whirlpool. Carlotta Walls, Jefferson Thomas, Ernest Green, Gloria Ray, Melba Pattillo, Terrance Roberts, Minnijean Brown, Thelma Mothershed, and Elizabeth Eckford were the nine students who were turned away that September 4, 1957. I applauded President Eisenhower who, after initially taking the stance of "wait and see," on September 25 sent in 1200 soldiers from the 327th Airborne Battle Group of the 101st Army Airborne Division to escort the nine African-American students into the school. One of the girls, Minnijean Brown, later was kicked out of school when she dumped her bowl of chili on the head of a heckling, taunting student. The Black cafeteria workers clapped at her shocking "retaliation." Imagine the momentary release/relief of the workers who felt as "second class" citizens, that they "had to take it." Minnijean Brown was transferred to New Lincoln High School, in NYC. In 1958, Ernest Green would be the first Black student, in a class of 602, to graduate from Central High. No one clapped for him as he walked across the stage with his diploma.

On September 10, 2007, dear *hermano* Dave Van Etten sent me an article from the *San Jose Mercury News* about the ongoing relationship between Melba Pattillo and Marty Sammon, one of the paratroopers commissioned by President Eisenhower to protect the nine Black high school students. Marty had been Dave's teammate on the University of Santa Clara's boxing team. Marty and Melba sometimes get together to "share their time in history," when Melba was fifteen and Marty was twenty-three. Melba speaks of her appreciation of the soldiers who protected her for six weeks. Melba says: "I celebrate this man every day of my life." Melba is now sixty-five and the head of the Communications Department at Dominican University in San Rafael, California. Melba Pattillo recalled how she had talked to her grandmother about Mahatma Gandhi's philosophy of non-violent resistance. She recounts the feeling of being protected at the high school: "The troops are here. We are going to live; we're going to make it." Marty volunteers as a boxing referee and even had a part in Clint Eastwood's film, *Million Dollar Baby*. He is also a stockbroker. Seventy-three years old, he said of the nine Little Rock students: "I'm filled with enormous respect for those kids. None of them quit."

Dorothy Counts Scroggins (born in 1942) was one of the Black students on September 4, 1957 first attempting to de-segregate Harry Harding High School, Charlotte North Carolina. The teachers ignored her in the classroom, not acknowledging her when she raised her hand. After four days of taunting, students' spitting in her lunch and other acts of harassment, Dorothy's parents withdrew her from school. Newspaper photos around the world showed White students humiliating Dorothy. James Baldwin eloquently, heartbrokenly wrote from Paris: *That's when I saw the photograph. Facing us, on every newspaper kiosk on that wide, tree-shaded boulevard in Paris were photographs of fifteen-year-old Dorothy Counts being reviled and spat upon by the mob as she was making her way to school in Charlotte, North Carolina. There was unutterable pride, tension, and anguish in that girl's face as she approached the halls of learning, with history, jeering, at her back. It made me furious, it filled me with both hatred and pity. And it made me ashamed. Some one of us should have been there with her.* Dorothy, a grandma and still an activist, says, "What happened to me on that day set me on a path. I've always wanted to work to

make sure that bad things don't happen to other children."
One of the buildings of Harry Harding High School is now
named after Dorothy Counts Scroggins.

****

In 1961, I read the controversial classic *Black Like Me* by
John Howard Griffin (1920–1980). To darken his skin
pigmentation to look like and be accepted as a Black man,
JHG took medicine orally, followed by massive exposure to
ultraviolet rays. Written "to shake up the status quo," it gave
me some feel for the social injustice Blacks suffered. At the
time, I was unaware of my mixed-race heritage, and I felt
Griffin, as a fellow White person, was confirming that racism against Blacks was real. Looking from today's perspective, I hold a more balanced view, appreciating Griffin's de-
served praise from Black supporters, including Dr. Martin
Luther King Jr. and Dick Gregory, but also considering his
Black critics who felt that he was patronizing, offensive, vo-
yeuristic, even exploitive. Griffin always knew he could return from receiving hate stares and discrimination (as a
"tenth-class citizen") to the security of White privilege. He
could not, though sympathetic, really know what it inescap-
ably meant to be a Black man at that time. Stokely Carmi-
chael (1941–1998), civil rights activist and Chairman of the
Student Nonviolent Coordinating Committee, observed
that "*Black Like Me* is an excellent book—for whites."

Griffin eventually stopped lecturing on his book, "finding it absurd for a White man to presume to speak for Black
people when they have superlative voices of their own."
Along with strong support, there were vindictive consequences for Griffin from racist Whites who wanted to vilify
him for his book. Once in 1964, he "was standing by the side
of the road in Mississippi with a flat tyre. He saw a group of

men approaching him. Griffin assumed the men were head-
ing over to assist him but instead they dragged him away
from his car and proceeded to beat him violently with chains
before leaving him for dead. It took Griffin five months to
recover from the assault . . . a particularly brutal form of literary criticism." ("Rereading: *Black Like Me* by John Howard Griffin," *The Guardian*, Sarfraz Manzoor, October 27,
2011) Though a national celebrity, JHG encountered continued hostile threats to him and his family. Hung in effigy,
he moved for safety from his hometown in Mansfield, Texas,
to Mexico for several years.

I have discussed *Black Like Me* over the years with students to arouse debate and insight. We share anecdotes.
There are students who say, "It's not like that anymore." But
another student, talking about a Black friend in NYC, relates
how difficult, in comparison to Whites, it is to hail a taxi.
"Yes better," he says, "but still. . . ."

Revisiting the story of JHG after so many years, I find it
an intriguing and relevant consideration of racism and, in
addition, it is like a revelatory bridge for me: Griffin from
White to Black to White, me from White to Black and
White. Furthermore, there is a unique connection between
Lionel Durand's WW II experiences and those of JHG. Like
Lionel, JHG was in Paris studying at the Sorbonne when the
war broke out, and he likewise joined the French Resistance.
He offered medical assistance to the Black Senegalese soldiers who were being used by the French Army as "cannon
fodder" against the Nazis. The Nazis treated captured Black
soldiers in the French Army horrifically. JHG was there and
a witness to this racist abuse. Griffin also helped Jewish refugees get out of France. He fought against racism by his courageous actions. Who knows, did Griffin cross paths with
Lionel at some point? Anything is possible!

****

In the next four chapters, I talk about the need for healing, individually and collectively. I could not fully welcome Lionel as my father until I had psychologically accepted and welcomed myself, celebrated myself—come what may—in a healthy way. I needed to feel comfortable in my own skin, sensitive to the boundaries and containment of my entire body-mind-heart-spirit.

The corona virus that causes COVID-19 is generating overwhelmingly strong emotions, fear, and anxiety for many of us undergoing challenging psychological and social effects. I hope, by analogy, my stories of personal and collective healing might be useful for those of us having a hard time, in whatever individual way we may experience it, needing to slow down, building and engaging inner and outer resources to reduce stress. We need each other more than ever. Together, as Greg Boyle says, we can tap "the power of boundless compassion" to take care of ourselves and each other.

3

Feeling and Healing the Primal Wound

According to 1985 statistics, although adoptees comprised 2–3% of the population, they represented 30–40% of the individuals found in residential treatment centers, juvenile halls, and special schools. . . . I call the primal wound, which is physical, emotional, psychological, and spiritual, a wound which causes pain so profound as to have been described as cellular . . . a wound caused by the separation from the biological mother, the connection to whom seems mystical, mysterious, spiritual and everlasting . . . we can no longer assume that babies are unaware or unfeeling . . . the child experiences the separation as abandonment, left helpless, hopeless, empty, and alone . . . adoptees repress feelings as if they can never count on anyone and must be self-sufficient . . . not only with a longing to find the lost object, but a longing to find the lost Self.
—Nancy Newton Verrier

My own history and appreciation of therapy started off with an intense two-year period from 1969–1971 when I was a volunteer assistant recreation therapist at Agnew State Mental Hospital in San Jose, California. I could sign up for workshops in San Francisco and Esalen Institute for volunteer/staff in-services (I considered training-therapy a prized "salary," which only a few of us took advantage of). I wanted to grow as a therapist and as a mentally healthy person. In the early 80s, I worked as a certified recreation therapist at El Centro Community Health Center in East Los Angeles where we were also offered in-services, but there was something foundational about my therapy from 1969–1971. In my year of intense trauma therapy in 2019, I went back to some of what I learned so many years ago and which I will now describe.

I did bio-energetic exercises with Alexander Lowen. I would strike large pillows with a tennis racket, screaming out "held-in" anger. I'd experience how tensions in my body had a strong emotional component; I breathed deeply into the tummy, expanding the stomach and lungs, breathing in and contracting chest and stomach breathing out. I put myself in touch with the energy moving in me and observed how movement and flow get clogged up by my over-thinking and neurotic emotional expression. The therapy made my conflicts obvious (some from childhood trauma) and facilitated a process of integration. It helped me be more emotionally healthy but was less than complete. I was asked to act out, move, dramatize, be aware of bodily reactions and contractions, to express feelings directly, to look others in the eyes, touch and be touched. I was releasing some "buried parts of me" that took up so much psychic energy. The basis was that the truth would make one free, so that I'd say to the therapist what I might say to my mother, my friend, or my own self—if only I could speak the truth of my feelings. I discovered I did not need to live up to others' expectations. I quieted, at least for the time, my own self-critical voice.

Perhaps the best therapy for me was just sitting in the hot tubs on the soothing shores of Big Sur, just being, quietly alone, deeply relaxed, outside in the dark, under the stars and wafting sea breezes. So, for two years, I would go to a variety of weekends at a very "laid back" but therapeutically intense setting, while I was volunteering in the extremely institutional milieu of Agnew State Mental Hospital. I did not feel so controlled by my need to be liked and to please, and by resentments underneath. I could say "no" as well as "yes" to projects without agonizing over possibly displeasing someone. I could more comfortably be with my ordinary relationships. Yet I had to admit there was still a hollow cavity in my heart of hearts.

✱✱✱✱✱✱✱✱

First, we just pay attention to our body, breathing, sensations, to see how we inappropriately—i.e., acting out a response from the past—become rigid and tight. We can naturally and organically acknowledge we have some responsibility to change, however slowly, our habitual tightening of our bodies. We get a sense of humor at how ridiculous it is what we do to ourselves, depriving ourselves of feeling fully the living organism. When I suppress my tears and pain, or when I put on a face to please or to attack, I tighten my mouth, lift my shoulders, gag my throat, and suppress or exaggerate breathing. If I do it often enough, I turn my face into a mask.

A telling episode of The Twilight Zone is the story of a father and his adult children at Mardi Gras. The father was soon to die, and the children were excitedly looking forward to possessing the father's rich inheritance. At the Fat Tuesday party, the children display their greed and envy as they jockey for position with Dad who was aware of their motivations, even though everyone had on a grotesque, gnarled mask. After the father died, the children could not remove their horrible masks—the true inner self now on the outer surface for all to see. They had to live with faces molded by masks. Therapy urged me to be whole, to radiate outwardly what is truly within. Hearts open, our masks easily fall off.

****

We all, in varying degrees, numb ourselves from pain, anger, joy, sexuality, fuller love relationships. Therapists aimed at encouraging the person to experience the self (some say "authentic self"), the whole organism, including voluntary and involuntary, superficial and profound levels of body-mind consciousness. They worked to undo the "contactlessness" of the person manifested in the individual's energy, breathing, and muscular armor. Through therapy, many of us were seeing how there could be a restoration of the natural movement of the life force. Alexander Lowen wrote: "A body is forsaken when it becomes a source of pain and humiliation instead of pleasure and pride."

There are different ways of looking at a person's character and personality. Therapists were demonstrating for us that our character can be observed in bodily presentation and attitude. We can experience in our own body where strong emotion is piled up within, let us say, in our shoulders, forming a tight ball around our necks, further "hanging us up" by hardened muscle mass. We can notice how open we are to the generous flow of life. We breathe, move, and emote to release the tensions in our body, allowing free expression of the previously "bound" energy we have inside. The first step of therapy—adapted toward varying needs— is learning to breathe easily and deeply. I expressed emotions by mobilizing and expressing them. If I needed to cry or be angry, then expression was allowed, short of violence. Deep breathing produces respiratory waves throughout the body. The life of the body is within its involuntary aspect, not only in its rational, conceptual expression. I have had to face how I handle threatening situations by hardening my-self. Some of this is necessary to survive, but as a chronic avoidance of feeling, it is like death. In my own therapy, I have observed a latent violence in myself which is being re-leased, relaxing my "hung up" shoulders, my own emo-tional-physical hang ups which lift me off the earth. Therapy gives me a sense of being grounded and alive, not just in my head.

****

Anyone can become angry—that is easy. But to be angry with the right person, to the right degree, at the right time, for the right purpose, and in the right way—that is not easy.
—Aristotle, Nicomachean Ethics

Anger builds on anger; the emotional brain heats up.
—Daniel Goleman

Some people, even therapists, encourage some kind of physical expression of anger, such as hitting pillows or a punching bag. While this might be appropriate for children, who have less self-control than adults, it usually doesn't work for adults in the long run. The one physical activity I might suggest for adults is a long walk, which will often restore perspective and lower the adrenaline and cortisol levels. Intense emotion dis-torts reality and judgment. A cooling off period is necessary.
—Nancy Verrier

Letting anger out, acting out in a non-destructive way, can be a useful catharsis for adults in therapy, but has a price and a limited usefulness and can be outgrown. The therapist should not goad someone into feeling anger. Expressing an-ger in an extreme way, even though non-destructive, can be unhealthy physiologically, our blood pressure and heart rate rising. Psychologically, venting may even feed anger. So, we must carefully consider, each in our own ways, how we relate to anger and rage, as well as finding suitable stress-reducing physical activities. "Allowing for the appearance of anger in a therapy-type setting where there is containment and control can be very helpful. Yet venting anger is often an excuse for poor anger management." (Nancy Verrier, *Coming Home to Self: The Adopted Child Grows Up,* p 71) In my own case, my therapist never prodded me to feel anger toward my mother. Rather I could hold anger within a wholistic attitude that anger and love can go together, that anger and other troublesome emotions can be observed in a witnessing, detached, restrained, paradoxical, and peaceful depth. Relating to anger without the need to act out made exercises such as punching large pillows obsolete. I don't deny or repress feelings but have found appropriate—even nourishing—ways of expressing the energy of anger and not projecting it at the wrong person, including myself.

In 2019, I again engaged in body-mind integrating exercises, though I did not do exercises acting out (even though in a safe environment and necessary for me as a young man) suppressed violence. I considered my therapy for trauma related to adoption as an interesting challenge, tender and respectful rather than as an intrusive burden, welcoming, transforming, integrating with some space and compassion troublesome thoughts and feelings.

✱✱✱✱✱✱✱✱

It's up to you—it's always up to you. You can deny, repress, distort, and bury your unresolved wounds all you want. You can re-frame them, pseudo-positivity them, detach from them, bypass them. You can re-name yourself, hide away in a monastery, turn your story around. And you can spend all your money on superficial healing practices and hocus-pocus practitioners. But it won't mean a damn thing if you don't do the deeper work to excavate and heal your primary wounds. The material is still there, right where you left it, subconsciously ruling your life and controlling your choices. This is the nature of unhealed material—it is alive, and one way or the other, it will manifest itself in your lived experience. It will language your inner narrative. It will obstruct your path and limit your possibilities. It lives everywhere that you live. And so, you have to decide—excavate it and bring it into consciousness where it can be worked through and integrated; or repress it and watch it rule your life. It's one of the hardest truths we have to face: If we don't deal with our stuff, it deals with us. There is no way around this. Choose.

—Jeff Brown, *Grounded Spirituality*

Nancy Newton Verrier signed my copy of her groundbreaking book, *The Primal Wound, Understanding the Adopted Child*, a book that refreshed me with life-changing insight and significant healing, inscribing: *Morgan, may your understanding of adoption be enhanced by this work. Best wishes, Nancy Verrier.*

Now, 42 years after my first intense therapeutic processes, extremely helpful but incomplete, I am confidently aware of my mixed racial makeup, truly more peaceful in relationship to my biological and adoptive parents, thanks in great part to the written and YouTube guidance of Nancy Verrier (admired advocate for children) who helped me understand my adoption. Nancy instructed me to be aware that coping behaviors are often the result of a traumatizing adoption, not the innate nature of the person who can thus overcome self-defeating behavior.

Severing the connection between the infant and biological mother causes a primal wound which often manifests in a sense of loss (depression), basic mistrust (anxiety), emotional and/or behavioral problems and difficulties in relationships with significant others, affecting the adoptee's sense of self, self-esteem, and self-worth throughout life. Loss and abandonment are imprinted on the unconscious of the adoptee which must be made conscious (accepted as real) and, at his or her good time, utilizing emotional and spiritual resources, integrated in the full spectrum of the personality. "Understanding, acceptance, empathy, and communication are the keys to the beginning of healing." (*The Primal Wound*, p. 109)

Adoptees have reacted normally to an abnormal experience of nonbiological families, living without an appreciation of their genetic makeup and a lack of mirroring (being reflected to by another of the same blood). We are mammals, meant to in all our senses be close to Mother during early years. For certain adoptees, the new mother does not pass the "sensory test" (do not feel, smell, sound right, missing a comfortable energy and resonance). "Every sensory aspect of the child expects *her,* knows *her,* wants *her.*" So, adoptees (and we must acknowledge the differences in individual adoptees) have to make conscious festering rigid wounds, which control us by our overreactions, and foster whole bodily-mental-spiritual healing.

The adoptee feeling perhaps that he really does not exist, and the birthmother that she does not have the right to exist, are the result of past experiences and should never be acted upon in the present. Therapy can loosen us from past traumatic memories. Nancy's work clarifies for us our right to flourish in the present without shame and undue grief or at the mercy of automatic, past reactions, the ability to hold both pain and joy in an integrated, nuanced personality that tolerates the very complex and paradoxical nature of living. "I believe that life is a paradox and that in order to avoid becoming frustrated and disillusioned, we have to accept this paradox (and perhaps even rejoice in it.) We have to accept that life is not made up of absolutes: black or white, dark or light, fair or unfair, but that in all aspects of life one will find elements of both black and white and myriad shades of gray in between." (*The Primal Wound,* p. 107)

The mother-baby is a unit, "an emotional, psychological, spiritual unit, whose knowing comes from intuition." Even if physically apart, mother and baby are psychologically bonded. I think this soul connection is at the root of my quest to know my biological parents that went past just curiosity and wanting to know their medical information. I wanted to recover a lost part of myself, a healthy and natural wanting to know my genetic identity. Since the child is relinquished at a beginning phase of development when "the mother not only plays the role of the child's Self but actually is that Self, we may not be dealing only with the 'primary love object', but with the loss of part of the Self. At that primal stage, the child's inability to mourn the loss of mother or of Self and his need to guard against further loss may cause him to adopt a false self." Anxiety overcomes a child who is insecure about the mother or mother figure's permanent presence; the wounded child might react aggressively or compliantly, but each, wishing for love and acceptance, has his or her fear of rejection and abandonment.

Adoptees may encounter the scared, fearful child inside. "Fear is the main reason that so many adoptees get stuck in their careers, their relationships, and their own personal growth. Beneath anger are fear and pain." (*Coming Home to Self,* p. 49) Many adoptees have a fear of abandonment (even staying in toxic relationships), of being disliked, of helplessness. We cannot be totally free of fear ("residue of trauma"), but we can relate to it differently by the practice of "allowing new patterns to form and become habitual." We can mature gracefully and joyously. Our brains can learn, our hearts surely can expand. We benefit by positively focusing our energy, creating new experiences, appreciating beauty, making friends, taking healthy risks, being concerned about others as well as ourselves.

"Unresolved grief over some long-forgotten (or repressed) loss may be at the root of much of that which is considered clinical depression in our society." (*The Primal Wound*, p.80)

✲✲✲✲✲✲✲

[H]ave patience with everything unresolved in your heart and try to love the questions themselves. . . . The point is to live everything . . . Live the questions now . . . live the way into the answer.
—Rainer Maria Rilke, *Letters to a Young Poet*

Angels sent me a loving wise therapist trained by Dr. Peter Levine, who developed Somatic Experiencing, instructing her that at the roots of trauma is the disconnection from our *felt* sense of belonging, that traumatic effects "stem from the frozen residue of energy that has not been resolved and discharged . . . we are instinctual beings with the ability to feel, respond, and reflect. . . . We don't confront trauma directly but work with its reflection, mirrored in our instinctual responses."

I was coached to resolve my trauma by learning to "move fluidly between instinct, emotion, and rational thought." My kind therapist's year-long concentrated therapy helped me become less stuck in the primal wound, not being controlled by it. She listened with interest and care as I talked about feelings, sensations, and thoughts that arose from finding my biological father (and earlier my biological mother) and ascertaining and sorting out the troubling circumstances surrounding my birth and adoption. I became conscious of long repressed aspects of myself, undigested pain, survival reactions of a child coping with a profoundly stressful event, still frozen in my adult nervous system. By accessing body memories, I would revisit but not relive my trauma. I accessed previously contracted energy, manifested by immobility (freezing) and incomplete-unintegrated fight or flight responses.

Dr. Levine says there are four components of trauma to some degree present in all who suffer trauma: hyperarousal, constriction, dissociation, and freezing (feeling helpless). Hyperarousal cannot be controlled voluntarily and is "primarily an indication that the body is summoning its energetic resources to mobilize resources against a potential threat." (Peter Levine, *Waking the Tiger, Healing Trauma*, p. 133)

Constriction (tension, tightening) is something we all experience when threatened, really or imagined, skillfully or neurotically. My therapy taught me to be more conscious and compassionate, understanding I could be grounded and connected. I considered how I could change my brain through the miracle of neuroplasticity, creating new neuro passageways, a tune up for my nervous system. Before traumatic experience from the past is healed, we can take our therapy as a life-magnifying adventure to feel and heal stress, mental and physical, exaggerated reactions, excessive self-centeredness, disconnection from heart and soul.

I can truly relate to Peter Levine's third component of trauma: dissociation. When I was living in gorgeous, humming San Francisco in the late 1970s, I dated and became for a short time the boyfriend of a vivacious, tall, energetic, free-spirited Mexican woman whose long black hair covered her entire back like a thick velvet blanket. She brought me to meet her large family who were impressed the gringo could speak Spanish. Once we organized a large party where each guest, whether Mexican or not, brought a special Mexican dish or two. We feasted on scrumptious guacamole salads, corn tortillas, rice, refried beans, burritos, pozole, chilaquiles, quesadillas, tacos, tostados, nachos, tamales, menudo, chicken with mole, chile relleno, enchiladas, churros and, of course, margaritas. After the party, eight or nine of us decided we would later go to a nightclub, where we had occasionally gone before to drink Jack Daniels, dance, make out, gab about work and dreams—promising or broken for the time being— and get into the music. My girlfriend said she would meet us in a couple of hours at the downtown club. When we arrived, to the shock of my friends, my girl-friend was on the dance floor, locked blissfully body to body, lost in kissing with "another" man. One of our friends went up to my girlfriend and tried to separate them and communicate we had arrived, but the couple were lost in each other. Because of unresolved fear of abandonment related to my adoption (now I know), it would have been too painful for me if the scene was *really* happening. Not grounded in/leaving my body, I denied what was right before my eyes.

"Because dissociation is a breakdown in the continuity of a person's felt sense, it almost always includes distortions of time and perception . . . out of our bodies. . . . Similarly, the woman being raped, the soldier facing enemy fire, or the victim of an accident may experience a fundamental disconnection from his or her body. From a corner of the ceiling, a child may watch him/herself being molested, and feel sorry for, or neutral toward, the defenseless child below, . . . enabling a person to endure experiences that are at the moment beyond endurance." (Peter Levine ,*Waking the Tiger*, p.137-38)

Peter Levine explains the last component of trauma: "Helplessness is closely related to the primitive, universal, biological response to overwhelming threat—the freezing response. If hyperarousal is the nervous system's accelerator, a sense of overwhelming helplessness is its brake . . . the body cannot move . . . when the threat is over, the intense helplessness and immobilization effects will wear off, but not completely. When we are traumatized, an echo of this feeling of being frozen remains with us . . . an overt reflection of the physiological process happening in the body."

I benefited from doing the exercise "Calling the Spirit back to the Body," building the bridge between body and mind: *For 10 minutes or so, take a gentle, pulsing shower in the following way: at a cool or slightly warm temperature setting, expose your entire body to the pulsing water. Put your full awareness into the region of your body where the rhythmical stimulation is focused. Let your consciousness move to each part of your body as you rotate. Hold the backs of your hands to the shower head then the palms and wrists then both sides of your face, shoulders, underarms, etc. Be sure to include every part of your body: head, forehead, neck, chest, back, legs, pelvis, hips, thighs, ankles, and feet. Pay attention to the sensation in each area even if it feels blank, numb, or painful. While you are doing this, say "this is **my** head, neck, etc. I welcome you back." Another similar awakening is to gently slap the different parts of your body briskly. Again, this will help re-establish a sense of a body with skin sensation when done regularly over time.* (Peter Levine, *Waking the*

Tiger, p 63) It is imperative that a person starting from a young age cultivate a sense of boundaries within the body with respect-honor for one's and others' personal and private space.

From the classroom of Girlie Laguerta de la Cruz, a teacher in Manila, Philippines, we can see via YouTube an example of how children's boundaries can be respected by giving the children the choice of how to greet the teacher in the morning. Girlie saw a 2018 video of a teacher (Mrs. Judy) in the US who created a chart for students to tap indicating whether they wanted to shake hands, hug, fist bump, elbow hello, dance. Girlie made her own chart for her students to indicate their preference for expressing good morning. A heart symbol = a hug; a hand with an open palm = a high five; two hands together = a handshake; a fist = a fist bump. The children choose what they feel comfortable with.

Once I went to lunch with a friend I had not seen for several years; he brought his 16-year-old daughter. We were all catching up on news when my friend scooted close to his daughter, putting his arms around her, kissing her on the cheek and saying how proud he was of her. But the daughter was cringing and embarrassed. She pushed her dad away saying, "Don't impose yourself on me; don't sit so close to me." My friend immediately apologized sincerely to his daughter and said thank you for reminding him how we can in our own neediness be disrespectful of the space of others. We ended up having a meaningful conversation and an enjoyable lunch that lasted two hours.

Understanding that trauma is biological, not just psychological, I paid attention to bodily sensations. I took time alone and with the therapist to do somatic and mindfulness exercises, becoming more skillful with regulating stress in my body including hyperaroused feelings of rage or depressed feelings. I sat in a chair with my feet on the floor. Placing my hands on my belly, the seat of life, feeling its expansion into the lungs (in breath) and contraction (out breath), I sensed the energy rising from the ground through my feet and legs to my belly, *a felt sense*, not a mental one. In another exercise, I exaggerated the polarity of strength-resiliency and collapse-defeat (incomplete response to threat). After entering fully into collapse, exaggerating my bad posture, and tightening of the belly, chest, and neck, I energetically shifted with my attention-breath-posture to reclaim an inner sense of strength and resiliency. I allowed my body to slowly turn in on itself and then straighten out, vertically aligning my back vertebra by vertebra, gradually starting with my lower back to my neck, elongating my head.

"Now imagine that there is an invisible thread at the top of your head, pulling you up to the sky, so that your whole vertebral column becomes even more elongated and extends upwards. Also, be aware of sensations in your chest, and see if there is a sense of openness or expansion, maybe even something you identify with pride." (Peter Levine, *Healing Trauma*, p. 63) I became sensitive to how conceptual, abstract thought, as important as it is, can block the freshness of immediate perception. I was less apt to get carried away by thought, stuck in my mind of the past and appreciated more the gift of fresh moment to moment living, so fleeting, multi-layered, and valuable.

I practiced a series of calming, gently restorative postures. Putting my left hand on my chest and right hand on my stomach, then placing my right hand on my forehead and left hand on my chest, and finally arms folded across chest, hands on shoulders, I would touch, hug, pat, tap, gently massage. I paid attention to changes in my breathing,

heartbeat, and sensations. When overtaken by a coping reaction of fleeing/fighting/freezing, I have been empowered
to access an inner "shift" that helps me respond rather than
simply react. Softening my belly, I could breathe with feeling
awareness melting anger and self-pity, stand up straight and
go to work. I found I could let my body-mind access positive, uplifting energy, a stronger appreciation of my natural
inner happiness, kindness, and patience. Somatic therapy
helped me (and is helping me) grow in compassion and acceptance for myself and others, enjoying the self-dignity of
having boundaries as now I am connected more solidly to
my body and more creatively-intuitively to my mind, nourishing a sense of sacred space within and around me, as well
as openness to others and to joyful experiences, to find the
light even in discouraging darkness, to be the best worthy
enough imperfect me.

My life continues as before, but I am carrying less emotional baggage; my mind, heart, and attitude are more enliv-
ened, appreciative, and at peace. In his book, *Going to Pieces
Without Falling Apart*, Mark Epstein describes that "shift" I
now find available in daily living: "Stillness does not mean
the elimination of disturbances as much as a different way
of viewing them . . . we get in trouble with anger if we try to
eliminate it through denial or avoidance, or if we turn it into
hatred. We do not confuse this inner 'let-come-what-comes'
practice to weaken our full human involvement in living.
We do not give up doing 'good' or resisting 'evil' in the
world, as if everything is fine the way it is."

4

Acompañamiento: Walking with Trauma Survivors

They walked the earth;
they walked the water;
they walked the air.
They were asked,
And why do you stand?
Because of the heart, they said,
and because of the children,
and because of the bread.
Because the cause is the heart's beat
and the children born and the risen bread.
—Dan Berrigan, SJ

To accompany someone is to go somewhere with him or her,
to break bread together, to be present on a journey with a be-
ginning and an end. There's an element of mystery, of open-
ness, of trust, in accompaniment. The companion, the accom-
panier, says: "I'll go with you and support you on your jour-
ney wherever it leads. I'll share your fate for a while—and by
"a while," I don't mean a little while. Accompaniment is
about sticking with a task until it's deemed completed—not
by the accompanier, but by the person being accompanied.
—Dr. Paul Farmer

*A*compañamiento, Spanish for "accompaniment," is a core orientation in Latin American liberation theology. It means accompanying, "walking with," walking in the company of those who are poor, displaced from their homes, or otherwise marginalized. This attitude is a counterbalance to paternalistic attitudes of "helping the poor" by providing needed resources, but not really getting involved in the lives of the people.

It is healthy and imperative that each of us lighten the burden of trauma to whatever degree we individually experience it. Yet we can be grateful for and must use our resources not only personally, but also for our communities and those communities (even internationally if we can) who suffered or suffer severe collective trauma.

Jean Donovan—a lay missionary serving and learning from, living with impoverished people in El Salvador—was one of four American churchwomen beaten, raped, shot in the head and dumped by the roadside by Salvadoran national guardsmen on December 2, 1980. Sisters Ita Ford, MM, Maura Clarke, MM, Dorothy Kazel, OSD and Jean, only 27 years old, were accompanying the disenfranchised during the bloody civil war. Considered subversives, they protested against the oppression of the heavy-handed junta and were feared as fomenting political rebellion. Jean had volunteered to work in El Salvador for two years through a church mission project. She was driving the bus in which she and the three nuns were riding when they were forced off the road, captured, and killed. Two weeks before she died as the violence raged all around her, Jean wrote to a friend in Connecticut: "The Peace Corps left today and my heart sank low. The danger is extreme, and they were right to leave. Now I must assess my own position because I am not up for suicide. Several times I have decided to leave El Salvador. I almost could, except for the children, the poor, bruised victims of this insanity. Who would care for them? Whose heart could be so staunch as to favor the reasonable thing in a sea of their tears and helplessness? Not mine."

I listened and conversed in Spanish with students who suffered the bitter consequences of being in the Civil War in El Salvador (1979–1992, claiming the lives of 75,000 people) which at the time was calling for and receiving at least some international support. I have visited El Salvador with heartfelt respect and love for the people; I heard about war-caused suffering, being shell-shocked, terrified of being killed. Insight into personal trauma can be extended to collective trauma, such as the trauma of racism, of extreme poverty, or the stress of violated boundaries a group or community might endure. Such communities who are victims of violence need to be listened to and offered resources to build family, friends, community, with professional, psychological, and spiritual help. It was as a community—as well as individuals—that Salvadorans suffered the agony of violence and so, as a supportive community, it had to heal that terrible shock and violation together.

****

"God saved me because he needed someone to tell the story of what happened."
—Rufina Amaya, *New York Times*, 1996.

I felt it a great honor and grace to interview Rufina Amaya (1943–2007), who told us how she was healing unspeakable trauma. "This is a story that can never be erased. No, the wounds to your heart can never be erased."

Rufina emanated an aura of genuinely bearing witness to an atrocity, while remaining peaceful and utterly human and humble. I loved Rufina right away when I first saw her. She had a special beauty, small boned, a round open face, crafted from unbearable suffering met by indomitable spirit. She fixed her hair, pulled back and up into a bun, which stuck straight up. She was slightly chubby; children seemed to be extremely attracted to her. She told us she just wanted to tell her story in quiet, righteous anger, calling for meaningful change. She exuded courage, simplicity, and nobility; her voice was strong, as she would speak before thousands of people at the protests against the School of the Americas. It was humbling to be in her presence.

Hidden behind a tree, Rufina Amaya witnessed as government soldiers raped women, then used machine guns to kill men, women, and children and setting their bodies on fire.

November 20, 1999, Fort Benning, Georgia

MZC: Thanks so much, Rufina. It's an honor to be with you. Sharing this little moment with you and wanting to support you. You are wonderful, a shining inspiration for us; I pray for you every day. When the December 11, 1981 massacre occurred at El Mozote, with its 809 victims, it was first denied by both the Salvadoran and American governments, despite what many community and church leaders were telling the world. You, being the sole survivor, had the courage to tell what happened in your village of twenty houses facing the community square. You have told this story now for eighteen years. In 1990, you were the first to testify in a criminal complaint against the Atlacatl Battalion (trained by American advisors) by Pedro Chica Romero of La Joya, a nearby hamlet to El Mozote. Pedro was a witness in his small hamlet to another killing of some of his relatives and neighbors by the Atlacatl Battalion. It was not until the El Salvador Peace Treaty of 1992 that an Argentine Forensic Anthropology Team was appointed by the United Nations to excavate the zone and finally begin exhumation. You have our admiration and love, Rufina. May I ask you about what motivates you to tell your heart-breaking story?

RA: I feel I am doing what God wants me to do, what I have all my desire to do. It is part of how I practice being a Catholic, not a separate activity. My story-telling and speaking with people come from my heart and also from my pain, my suffering the loss of my husband, Domingo Claros, who was twenty-nine; my son, Cristino, nine; and my three daughters Maria Dolores, five, Maria Lillian, three, and Maria Isabel, eight months. I cannot even cry anymore. It is true: my body produced so many tears that they are all gone. I speak to you; I speak for them, my family, my friends, and my neighbors who cannot speak any more. Even though I am a simple person, I use my voice so people will not forget what happened at El Mozote.

MZC: Just two more questions would be all right? What is your participation in the organized church? Do you consider yourself an "activist"?

RA: I am a lay pastor in the Catholic Church in El Salvador. My faith is very important as it gives me love, as do my family and friends. My religion gives me courage not to be afraid to speak out loudly, and my religion allows me to get refreshed spiritually. I like to lead "reflection groups," where we talk about the relationship of God to our own lives. I have had so many visitors from all around the world; I truly feel I am meant to talk, and I am happy and serious to talk. I do practice quiet prayer and have some reflection time also, but I would call myself an activist. I will never be quiet about what is right and what is wrong, what's unjust abuse, unjust murder against innocent, good people. I am publicly asking those responsible for the murders to publicly ask our pardon. Yes, I am an activist and also a Catholic. I am outspoken. I am not satisfied. Yet, I am a person of faith too, not only an activist.

****

I was in El Salvador in 1994 to remember the fifth anniversary of the violent passing (11/16/89) of six Jesuit priests from Spain (Ignacio Ellacuría, Amando López, Joaquín López y López, Ignacio Martín Baró, Segundo Montes, Juan Ramón Moreno). Elba Ramos and her daughter, Celina, were also summarily assassinated. Joan Didion, writing in 1982, paints the sad picture: "Terror is the given of the place. Bodies turn up in the brush of vacant lots, in the garbage, thrown in ravines in the richest districts, in public restrooms, in bus stations. Some are dropped in Lake Ilopango." I went to El Salvador to touch and be touched by the land and its people, to cry for brothers and sisters who have suffered, to try to understand and learn with reverence. And cry for myself, for my own tolerance for violence. I asked many how could politics-power-government, conceived to serve the people, to "en-right" and enrich all, become such a destructive repression and death machine?

El Salvador is a wonder: lovely distant hills, rich varieties of vegetation, city marketplaces, refreshing ocean, and sure, great people, a wounded, but strong, determined people. I said a prayer at the memorial of the murdered Jesuit padres and for Elba and Celina Ramos who died with them. In the early morning of November 16, 1989, at the UCA University (Universidad Centro Americana), around 2:30 a.m., six Spanish Jesuit priests were ripped from their beds and executed. Their housekeeper, Elba, and her daughter Celina were also assassinated. There were about three hundred officers and enlisted men at the UCA campus on the night of the murders. The UCA had been bombed in April and July of 1989. The death squad wrote "FMLN" (rebel guerillas) on the walls to escape blame. In January of 1990, eight men were arrested for the murders, six from the Atlacatl Battalion and two officers of the military academy. Two men were convicted, Col. Benavides of seven murders, Lieutenant Mendoza of the murder of Celina Ramos. They were sentenced for thirty years. The provincial of the Jesuits in El Salvador, Fr. Tojeira, officially asked for pardon for the two convicted men, because he stated those who ordered the attack were not brought to trial. Both men were set free. On May 30, 2011, a Spanish court found twenty members of the Salvadoran military guilty of murder, terrorism, and crimes against humanity.

The Jesuits had openly favored a peace accord among the political factions in the country. Some of the military wanted to continue hateful polarities, especially by propagating that the Jesuits were only supporting the guerrillas. The Jesuits, in fact, were imploring for the integration of the varied political and economic elements in Salvadoran society. Father Ellacuría and President Christiani, with all their ideological differences, were both talking about how they could unite energies to give to the promising peace accord. Many human rights groups say this is the reason far right elements killed Fr. Ellacuría and his friends. The Jesuits favored agrarian reform and the end of political repression that stifled a sharing of power. Some Jesuits, such as Rutilio Grande, and other community leaders had spoken out for the poor, as well as for all elements in the society, political and economic. They were teaching principles of how to use and share resources, no matter what one's wealth or political belief might be. They spoke openly for social justice, human rights and against political terror. On March 24, 1980, after three years as archbishop of San Salvador, Óscar Arnulfo Romero (born 1917) was gunned down while saying Mass. Now I see pictures of bloody, mashed bodies of the six Jesuits and two women. I wanted to feel the sublimity of the soul and its inviolable spark; but I only saw profanely violated corpses.

I was welcomed in the home of a former student whose father—a "casualty" of the civil war—was now in prison. She said many of her friends no longer would speak to her. Yet she spoke so lovingly of her "disgraced" father, how when she was a little girl, she and her father would dig for clams, lying buried, like gray fruit in the moist sand. "He believes in speaking up for civil rights and justice." I was inspired by peaceful activist organizations and individuals. I listened to high-school and college students and found the spirit of activism and volunteering alive in people of all ages. I do not consider activism or volunteering as special; it is very natural and rewarding for ourselves, as well as offering needed help to a carefully considered cause. Activism's engine is revved by confidence in human beings' resourcefulness (when really wanting some change).

✱✱✱✱✱✱✱✱

In 2001, I was invited by Luis Arriaga, SJ, lawyer and Jesuit scholastic, to visit with him in Chiapas. For many years, Bishop Samuel Ruiz (1924–2011) labored to defend the human rights of the Indigenous in Mexico and especially in Chiapas, Mexico's southernmost state. He was fluent in Tzotzil and Tzeltal, the region's two most important Indigenous languages, and *con gran gusto y respeto a todos*, he served for 40 years in Chiapas before he resigned on his 75th birthday on November 3, 1999. "The Indigenous peoples understand that they have to recover their cultural identity, or to live it if they have already recovered it. They also understand that this is not a favor or a concession, but simply their natural right to be recognized as belonging to a culture that is distinct from the Western culture, a culture in which they have to live their own faith." Just as a person heals her own trauma, so collective members of a culture must break free of the gnawing discrimination and violations against their human rights to a culture worthy of fair regard and cooperation. I think of Samuel Ruiz, this friend and bishop of the poor, welcoming Indigenous to express their voice and build inner and communal resources. Samuel Ruiz's spirit reminds me of Rumi: "I am so small. I can barely be seen. How can this great love be inside me? Look at your eyes: they're small, but they see enormous things."

Before my trip to Chiapas, close friends Dutch (Raising Hell in Heaven and Enjoying it) and Juanita Schultz, asked me to deliver some money to one of the women they befriended in Chiapas. "She has suffered unspeakable indignities but is a strong leader in her community. She helps the poorest of the poor. We understand each other, this lovely woman and her doting grandpa and grandma from the States; we know each other in our shared humanity; we learn from each other in a closeness which turned to respectful love developed over many years." Dutch and Juanita visited the Tzotzil (Mayan) Indians of Chiapas each year, sometimes two or three times, bringing financial and moral support to Padre Pedro Arriaga, SJ, and the Jesuits who were responsible for serving the large and politically charged district of Chenalho, including three compounds where the survivors of the 1997 Acteal massacre reside. Dutch and Juanita were instrumental in helping a Mayan gentleman receive a specialized operation in the US. At that time in 2001, paramilitaries still prevented the Tzotzil Indians from returning to their fertile land in Acteal. They continued to live in a small compound in Acteal with bare necessities and land impossible to till. The Blue Cross of Mexico brought one meal a day to the Indigenous people, but the US Red Cross found that nine percent of the children under age five suffered from malnutrition.

✶✶✶✶✶✶✶✶

Ideas of the Mexican Revolution's social shaking, a hundred years ago, still reverberate in Chiapas: wanting the sharing of land, resources, dignified work; appreciation for Indigenous culture-religion-customs; nurturing-educating children; addressing the traumatic stress imposed over the years through discrimination towards the Indigenous, changing from the exploitation of the poorest into an inclusive "fair-trading" giving and taking of goods and services. Chiapas has a population of four million (37% Indigenous), a land of spectacular flowers, lakes, plants, rivers, hills, volcanoes, thick jungles, and forests producing mahogany and rosewood. Tourists come here to see the Mayan archaeological sites of Palenque, Bonampak, Izapa, and Yaxchilan. On a cool, softly rainy evening I took in the sights and sounds in Parque Central de San Cristóbal, Chiapas. The Mexican Marine Corps, snappily uniformed, full orchestra and chorus, were singing their guts and hearts out: operatic songs and ballads of the Revolution such as "Adelita" (with blackest long hair to whom the revolutionary will return breathing liberty and make beautiful, breath-taking love). The park is packed, yet children still find space to jump for glee as the choir's full loud voice shakes a giant banner of two doves about to kiss as they are perched in the blue skies. *Todos a la Feria de la Primavera y de la Paz.* Come Everyone to the Spring Fair of Peace. Violins, singing, tears touching so much pain and suffering and loves, the aliveness of buoyant emotion. Sweets, popcorn, steamed corn on the cob, dancing, waving, flirting. *Esperanza.* Hope for economic and social tranquility.

****

Luis Arriaga took me to visit Acteal and Las Abejas (the Bees), a peaceful group of Tzotzil Indians organized in 1992. Although they intellectually supported the Zapatistas, these Indigenous would never involve themselves actively or militantly with either the Zapatistas or the multiplicity of religious and political disputes rampant in many areas of Chiapas. They believe their peace-filled lives should be the honey that heals collective and personal trauma. Catholics, Presbyterians, and Baptists meet, work, and pray together for peace. Jesuits sent small groups of Tzotzil Indians into Guatemala to attend sensitivity sessions conducted by a Jesuit psychologist. They returned to the Acteal and Chenalho districts to conduct workshops and healing circles. These gentle, impoverished Indians not only deserve nutritious meals and medical aid during their displacement, but also the chance to truly heal and enjoy greater harmony in their families and communities.

Sensitivity sessions are group therapy and were used by the Indigenous leaders—in a gentle, supportive way, far different from some of the sessions I heard about in the United States. The "client-centered" group therapy offered safe environments (with a caution not to use bullying or undue confrontation) to allow trauma survivors—reflecting back and forth to each other and all—to work out their issues verbally, emotionally, physically on a deep calm level. Listening to others and trusting that one will be listened to without judgmental imposition were emphasized. An Indigenous facilitator of a sensitivity group said that at some gatherings all just cried, hugged, and consoled each other. People were not forced to open up and be "honest" but the welcoming, accepting, compassionate group energy cultivated a natural openness at the comfortable level of each individual. Being listened to evoked the desire to speak and share when the time was right. Aggressive breaking down of social barriers was not allowed. Aware of the fragile boundaries of a traumatized people, the leader and the group encouraged being in touch with feelings and, as one gained insight, taking responsibility for one's own and communal healing. "You are worthy; we are here not to make each other defensive and uncomfortable, but to allow our nature to shine more brightly."

We drove to Acteal on windy roads in an old Nissan pickup, at times along green forests, people scurrying with wood tied to their backs or pushing goats. Las Abejas community in Acteal are "displaced," peaceful revolutionaries, organizing for social justice, and were still a mourning community because of the massacre on December 22, 1997 of 45 of their members, an attack by rightwing paramilitaries who surrounded their community from 11:30 a.m. to 6:00 p.m. Ernesto Paciencia (secretary of the Acteal community) showed me the makeshift chapel where so many, praying and fasting for peace were killed and the hilly gorges where people fled, a pregnant young woman stripped, violated, baby cut from her womb. Exactly 45 bodies are buried in two layers in a concrete edifice, where Ernesto shows me pictures on the walls of the deceased, including his mother and sister. We sit quietly for several minutes. Tears cannot hide. Darling, bashful Zenaida, now holding hands so tenderly with *abuelita*, is one of the fifty children orphaned: she is blind from taking a bullet to the head. Luis comments that the people still carry traumatized, unhealed hearts, and that we must accompany them to recover and stand proud among themselves without fear, building upon their cultural richness and inner goodness as unique individuals.

Later we went to a wake in the mountains for the community's friend, Victoriano, our Nissan pickup sometimes sliding backwards, a newly purchased coffin sticking out diagonally in the back. A few droopy horses stare at us when we finally deliver the coffin to a large community, some weeping around the corpse of their Victoriano, friend, relative, husband and father. He was 52. As Luis wryly says, "He died of poverty." Many men wear white tunics; three men play a plaintive melody: a violin, a guitar, and a harp. The blanket-covered corpse is placed in the wooden coffin with some of Victoriano's belongings and a few peso coins. We smell unavoidable death and the life and humanity around it. Before we leave, we are offered and eat with gusto corn tortillas with beans, cooked over an open fire.

****

As a result of meeting a few times in Los Angeles with Pastor John Rutsindintwarane, a native Rwandan, I came to appreciate "person to person" Pastor John's dedication to Rwanda. How can one grapple with the 1994 disastrous slaughter of human beings? Bill Clinton said that the biggest regret of his presidency was not stopping the one-hundred-day killing of eight hundred thousand people by ethnic majority Hutu extremists (85% of the population) who exterminated without restraint 75% of rival minority Tutsis as well as any of their political opponents or Hutus who tried to protect Tutsis.

Through organizing, Pastor John wants to add to positive, empowering healing, uplifting energy to the marvelous

people of Rwanda. He spoke to me of the beauty and determination of his people whose hearts were seared with unspeakable grief. John began organizing in Rwanda in 2006
after a one-year internship with the US Faith in Action affiliate Oakland Community Organization in Oakland, California. For Pastor John, the devastating effects of the 1994 genocide and the overwhelming barriers faced by the survivors
fueled his search for tools to rebuild his country.

Faith in Action Rwanda was born in a small, all-but-for-
gotten part of southeast Rwanda called Mumeya, a stone's
throw from the Tanzanian border. Pastor John was invited
to work in this village. He told Mumeya residents that he
had no money to offer, but that he was willing to share his
brain and his heart. Mumeya villagers from five different
congregations began leadership training in a grassy area under a big tree, a welcoming space open to everyone. Community leaders started holding one-to-one conversations to
identify the major needs in the community. Mumeya residents decided that a health center was their top priority.
They organized their own labor and resources, gathered
supplies and medical staff from public officials, and in 2009
after the completion of three rooms, they opened their first
fully functioning health center. Pastor John believes that
lasting improvements are dependent upon Rwandans working side-by-side, developing capacity as they take on critical
community needs, envisioning a future Rwanda where
Rwandans are equipped with the skills to solve problems
they face and lead happy, wholesome lives. Over 10 years,
Rwandan leaders have generated public improvements and
services for 120,000 people. Projects include two health clin-
ics, three schools, three new homes, secure water access,
electricity, a welding school, a community center, a roofing
tile business, reforestation, and road construction. John

Baumann in admiration says: "You are helping people write their own story of success."

A smiling Mumentwarri Juvenary, 87, recently told Pastor John: "Man, when you came to my house the first time, I thought you came to convert me to join your religion. I did not want to tell you that I don't believe in these mushrooming churches with their pastors who promise us many things that never happen. Here at Nyarubuye/Nyabitare, we have six small buildings of churches, but we did not have a single medical clinic. I keep watching you training people under the trees, then putting training in action. This is what we need. A healthy mind and body go to church. I am so excited to see the first clinic in our villages. Our families will no longer walk seven kilometers to the nearest medical clinic."

On April 6, 2019, an Associated Press News article by Ignatius Ssuuna talks about some of the reconciliation going on in communities of Rwanda where survivors and perpetrators may live side by side. "Twenty-five years ago, Tasian Nkundiye murdered his neighbor with a machete. The 43-year-old Hutu and a few other men from his Rwandan village chopped a Tutsi man to pieces. Nkundiye was convicted of the killing and other crimes and spent eight years in prison. Today he lives near the widow of the man he killed. And somehow, they are friends—their children and grandchildren play and share lunch together, their cows graze in the same field. 'I am very grateful to her,' Nkundiye, now 68, said of the widow, 58-year-old Laurencia Mukalemera. 'Ever since I apologized to her after prison life, confessing to my crimes and asking her for forgiveness, she has accepted me. I even leave my children with her when I am away.'"

****

Over the years I have spoken (sometimes helped by an interpreter, usually a younger member of the family) with Cambodian students who had lived under the ruthless Khmer Rouge and the tyrant Pol Pot (1975–1979). They survived through constant fear, hunger, sickness, imprisonment, torture, forced labor, killings of family members and friends, and the unspeakable torment of genocide. They told me how the government demanded a passive and subservient role from them. One had to pretend to be foolishly naïve and ignorant, demeaning the value of the individual human being and her/his thirst for freedom. Cambodians could not wear eyeglasses or use an educated and polite form of speech. Children who reported parents' transgressions were given more food. Buddhism, the principal religion for 90% of the Cambodians, was harshly dismantled and forbidden to be practiced. The government sought total control by destroying the trust within the family; it forcibly separated children from their parents.

Between October 1979 and May 1980, 164,000 Cambodian refugees arrived in Thailand. During the cruel Khmer Rouge's reign, 1.7 million–2.5 million Cambodians, a fourth of the entire population (eight million), were executed or died from forced labor, disease, and starvation. Through their tragic and catastrophic accounts and their dreams for a brighter future as well, my students (who certainly were also my teachers) inspired me with their enthusiasm and resilience. They told me how they esteemed education for their children, grandchildren, great-grandchildren, nieces, and nephews. They wanted to have a happy life in America. Doesn't our love and care for the younger generation in all cultures make the world go 'round? One of my students for three years was an eighty-year-old man, a father of six, grandfather of fifteen. Many from his immediate family had been slaughtered in Cambodia, and he related to me he had unsettling, recurring dreams, which caused him to wake up covered in sweat. He would enter the classroom and bow to me. He exuded a feeling of gentleness, yet an underlying strength, a sense of dignity, somehow functioning well by focusing his energy on his present life and continuing his Buddhist meditation and mindfulness practice to help alleviate post-traumatic suffering. I would bow to him as well.

5

Kinship of the Heart

If we don't learn to embrace our own wounds, we will be tempted to despise the wounded. We cover our wounds. And we all have them. The destructive coping behavior that leads to someone's arrest is almost always an extreme form of numbing, running from or expressing incredible past trauma. While the justice systems create separation and punishment to try and deter such behavior, the wounds in our community go unhealed. The most wounded become the most disposed of.
—Father Gregory Boyle, SJ

When people do not know they are loved, a cold black hole forms in the psyche, where they start to harbor beliefs that they're insignificant, unimportant, or lacking in beauty and goodness.
—John Welwood

Padre Boyle, treasured friend and founder in 1988 of Homeboys Industries, freely gives hugs and smiles of unconditional love and acceptance, offering "extravagantly tender" kinship to former gang members and former prisoners and to many others such as me. I first met Greg many years ago at Dolores Mission, a Catholic church in Boyle Heights where Greg lived. I was teaching ESL once a week to homeless men who were sleeping in the church. Bob Holstein (whom you'll meet in Chapter 8) had showers installed so the guests could shower every day as well as receive other services, with healthy participation and support of parishioners and the good Sisters across the street at Dolores Mission School. Greg is a phenomenon, a man for others, a guru (bringing light to darkness), a contemporary contemplative in action, a humorous, thoughtful man of good heart and wise mind.

My favorite place to have lunch with friends is Homegirl Cafe with its energetic, attentive staff. Powerful paintings take turns being displayed on the cafe walls, creative displays of shapes-shades-lines-imaginings, for example, depictions of Indigenous ancestors richly colored on canvas, side by side with mesmerizing bold images from the *barrios* of East Los Angeles.

I am most grateful to Greg for listening to and responding with blessings to my story of Lionel Durand, *Revelation and Healing*. Over the years I have enjoyed visits with Greg, catching him by chance in his office, taking phone photos, together sharing a warm appreciative hug. Both Catholics, we at the same time share an interest in Buddhism. Greg has been called a Jesuit Buddhist, and he says *yes,* that is true. The Dalai Lama asserts there is no exception: *all in essence have Buddha Nature.* Greg urges us (as he models by his actions and attitude) to treat others as we want to be treated. Magnify the experience of intuiting/perceiving the inner goodness of each person: *all most basically have unshakable goodness.* We do not save Homies, we *see* Homies. We see because all of us, with patience, at heart can mine inner wholeness in ourselves and can see that same "divine" spirit-essence in others. We can speak our "whole language," which includes the mystic's perception of soul, inter-being, inclusion, loving-kindness, compassion, and careful discernment. Our dignity, our "Buddha Nature" is never in question; *only our access to it is.*

The motto at Homegirls and Homeboys, "Nothing stops a bullet like a job," has evolved to "Nothing stops a bullet like a healing heart." On an online August 10–11, 2020 conference, I caught up with some of the women and men at Homeboys, open during the pandemic as an "essential" service. Father Greg, magnanimous heart, G, sets up a makeshift "outdoor" office open at nine in the morning, with some lining up as early as 7:00 a.m. The remarkable, loving and lovable, capable staff and volunteers continue their services. I was moved by the Zoom presentations of former gang members, former prisoners who made good use of the services of Homeboys Industries, and now they were serving others, telling stories of "pain carried around" and thus wanting to numb oneself, incidents of violence and what it does to your body and spirit, and hopeful transformative shifts, appreciative tears coming out, letting go of self-imposed burdens, changing from wanting to hurt and pay back others to wanting good for others and for oneself, in this together. Carisma, a former prisoner who was imprisoned when only 14 years old, said he took advantage of Homeboys and "got bitten by love." Victor, now happy, told how he rose from the ashes of a deeply traumatic life, born into a culture of gangs, violence, and anger. At eight years of age he was given a gun to shoot out streetlights so the gang in the dark could sell Shermans, tobacco or marijuana cigarettes dipped in PCP. "I had so much hate; I never said 'I love you.' I am transforming into a man who loves." Victor's talk, like Carisma's and others', set the tone and depth of the conference.

Standing with the demonized means allowing the world to see not faceless gang members but individuals who are sons and daughters, mothers and fathers, brothers and sisters. It means forgiving and letting go of past transgressions and

looking forward without judgment. . . . We believe that heal-
ing happens in an irresistible culture of relational tenderness.

Homeboys has become a bustling, well-organized mag-
net for disenchanted gang members (120,000 gang members—1100 gangs—in Los Angeles County). Homeboys Industries offers social enterprises which serve as job-training:
electronic recycling, baking, Homegirl Cafe, Catering, Silk-
screen & Embroidery, Homeboy Gear, City Hall Diner, Gro-
cery, Online Market, and Farmer's Market. Some earnestly
want to "look in the mirror and make that change," go beyond gangs and prisons and avail themselves of free services
and programs: Tattoo Removal, Workforce Development,
Educational Services, Homeboys Art Academy, Mental
Health Services/Anger Management/Trauma Healing, Domestic Violence, Legal Services, Substance Abuse, and Case
Management. One is invited to complete an 18-month program to access and put into daily life these valuable resources, inner and outer, to discover and inhabit one's authentic, grounded, whole self.

Greg told the story of a prisoner, Louie the Photo
Bomber, always getting in on group photos when he had the
chance. One day G was visiting Louie and others; sure,
enough Louie, uninvited, inserted himself in a few photos.
That day a concert pianist was going to perform for the in-
mates and some visitors. The concert was captivating, exhilarating, heart opening, all were sobbing. After the concert
Louie asked Greg *why* the musician would play for prisoners
like *him?*

Because you are worthy of beauty and music.

"And so, the voices at the margins get heard and the circle of compassion widens. Souls feeling their worth, refusing

to forget that we belong to each other. No bullet can pierce this. The vision still has its time, and, yes, it presses on to fulfillment. It will not disappoint. And yet, if it delays, we can surely wait for it." (Gregory Boyle, *Tattoos on the Heart,* p. 212)

On June 23, 2020, the Homeboys and Homegirls were visited by Prince Harry and Meghan Markle who volunteered at the bakery. "The Duke and Duchess of Sussex were just 'Harry and Meghan' to the Homies. The staff was honored they took the time to see us, hear us, and walk on our journey today. We will never forget it. . . . They rolled up their sleeves and deeply engaged with our workers in the Bakery and Cafe. It was immediate kinship and heartening in its mutuality." Meghan, along with her mom, had first met Gregory Boyle twenty years ago when she participated at Homeboys in a cooking workshop.

Homeboy Industries CEO, Thomas Vozzo commented: "With their visit, the Duke and Duchess of Sussex saw the dignity and power that comes from having a job. At Homeboy, through the social enterprise businesses, people can continue to heal, and they work, learning skills and changing their lives, changing their families, and changing their communities."

In addition to her support of animal rights, Meghan has spoken out in favor of peaceful protest (looting and vandalism hurt people and the cause) against the terrible killing of George Floyd and other blatant injustices. "I wasn't sure what I could say to you," she said in a speech. "I wanted to say the right thing and I was really nervous that I wouldn't or that it would get picked apart, and I realized the only wrong thing to say is to say nothing. Because George Floyd's life mattered, and Philando Castille's life mattered, and

Tamir Rice's life mattered, and so did so many other people whose names we know and do not know." (*Today*, June 24, 2020, Alexander Kacala and Diana Dasrath)

****

The work of the mature person is to carry grief in one hand and gratitude in the other and to be stretched large by them. How much sorrow can I hold? That's how much gratitude I can give. If I carry only grief, I'll bend toward cynicism and despair. If I have only gratitude, I'll become saccharine and won't develop much compassion for other people's suffering. Grief keeps the heart fluid and soft, which helps make compassion possible.
—Francis Weller

For thirty-five years, in collaboration with others (sometimes solo), especially with lasting friendships with staff and former staff members of Matraca and Vivir Joven and Mexican Jesuits, I have visited and interacted with poor working street children (some *living* on the streets) in Veracruz and Chiapas. Some were orphaned; some abandoned; some runaways, usually from abuse; some with dangerous addictions; some prostituting themselves; some with physical and mental challenges; many traumatized; all lovable and worthy of our concerned regard. On a few occasions, a young tearful child would say, "Please adopt me." It broke my heart; I reflected how fortunate I was to be adopted by parents who gave me material and spiritual benefits through which, as an adult, I could live a happy life among its trials and tribulations and reminders of imperfectness. Yes, I truly needed the healing for personal wounds I have described. But imagine these children, listen to them speaking from the bitterly cold and stressful condition of vulnerability on the street, a cry from a child, desperate and lost. It's our natural calling, together, being influencers in our global community, to help poor children, with moral and financial support as best we can by giving energy to the movers and shakers bringing care and empowerment to the disadvantaged, our less fortunate sisters and brothers. I think most of us resonate with all children, and so can likewise feel these street children's eyes, hearts, and spirits communicating: *love us, treasure us, keep us safe and healthy, educate us, guide us with affection and instill in us the essential principles of living a fully engaged, meaningful life.*

Matraca is an acronym for Movimiento de Apoyo a Trabajadores de la Calle (Services for Working Street Children), an organization based in Xalapa, Veracruz. Matraca means "noise-maker," a wooden toy that Mexican children use to celebrate and play. It makes a raucous, clacking noise. I imagine it represents children's lively expressions of spaciousness and sacred boundaries together, and glee-freedom to explore and discover. Hooray! Let loose! Whirl a matraca! Dance. Laugh. Be free to grow, dear young human flower. That is our metta for you, our heartfelt wish that you be well, happy, being in supportive and loving circumstances where you can grow and blossom.

Matraca was started in 1991 by a Jesuit priest, David Fernández, and then directed by another Jesuit, Juan Francisco Kitazawa, as part of the University of Veracruz community's outreach to these children. Josefina Castrejón Holguin is now the director. Its purpose is to provide social, educative, and formative assistance for child and adolescent workers, some living on the street. Former director Octavio Diaz: "From the weakest we have learned that the hope for an ever more just world is a task that we must all face together in order to create it; it's a gamble on brotherhood, on humanity; a gamble on love." Xalapa signifies "sandy waters" in

Nahuatl. It is in the center of the state of Veracruz, ancestral land of the Olmecs, Totonacas, Chichimecas, Toltecas, and Teochichimecas, the birthplace of Mexico's pre-Colombian cultures, still lightly whispering to us through ancestors and ancient art. The lovely, jagged peaks of Sierra Madre Oriental dominate the landscape of western Veracruz. Rolling green foothills unveil fields of flowers, rich coffee beans, *animalitos, gente genial.*

It was in the nearby gray-cool harbor of Veracruz that Hernán Cortés cast down his aggressive anchor in 1519, going on from there to conquer the Aztecs. Now the state of Veracruz is a 450-mile stretch, a multi-colored-blended tapestry of seven million people, many of them Indigenous (the third largest population of people who speak Indigenous languages), with a mixture of Spaniards, Africans, Italians, Greeks, French, and Cubans. Some three thousand years ago, the Olmecs predominated here, a sophisticated race that created their own mathematics, religious myths, and calendar, which was later adopted by the Aztecs and the Mayas. They were master carvers of giant basalt heads, nine to ten feet tall, nine to ten tons in weight, with large-lips and broad-noses and facial expressions that seem to express a faint disapproval. Today at the port of Veracruz, at that magical moment of sunrise: barest light on hundreds of eager boats pushing into the sea, waters gradually illuminated by pinks and oranges, dabbled on oil-rig-shadowed silvery water, fresh esperanzas for an abundant catch. . . . And into the evening, lively marimba bands, danzón, cervezas, seafood, giggling-joyfully shrieking children, a beggar—lifted for a delicious moment from his squalor—entranced by rhythmic-sensual rounds of dancing in the sweating plaza.

The working kids in Xalapa pass hours in the streets selling gum, cleaning car windshields, flagging down taxis, begging—sometimes as clowns and jugglers. They spend a lot of time trying to stay one-step ahead of the Seguridad Publica whose officers try to get them out of the streets. Most of the children maintain a bond with their families. Yet about 150 of Xalapa's three thousand working children have no home, no place to learn their ABCs, or get their meals or any kind of medical care. Street children, working kids, and homeless young people here sometimes sell their bodies to survive. According to unsettling government statistics, some 16,000 Mexican minors prostituted themselves in 2020; six of ten are boys. Some 60 percent of them are victims of sexual abuse; half have drug problems. Abusive pimps inject some of them with anabolic steroids to increase their sexual attractiveness. Ten percent are HIV positive. Five percent are teen moms.

From my journal: It is Easter week, and I am at Matraca's downtown facility of classrooms, offices, medical dispensary, kitchen, and showers. Young teens Omar, Miguel, and Juan talk to me about their lives on the streets. They play fútbol and basketball with other children in Matraca's outside patio. I enjoy joining the games with a small audience cheering us on. One of the boys, drying off from a shower, pops his head out, hair over his eyes, like a seal emerging at sea-surface. Roberto, hoping for tips, washes windshields at a nearby traffic intersection. He tells me how he and four other youngsters were recently detained for three days as a "traffic menace." I have a short talk with Angela Muñoz who works in an agrarian movement with Indigenous people, helping farmers get access to water, tools, and quality seeds. Angela says they want to be self-sufficient and how she admires the quiet dignity that informs their organizing together. I visit with Lara, a vivacious, bright two-year volunteer from Spain who takes university students to assist and learn from outlying barrios.

One soon-to-graduate student told me about his three years of volunteering: "You know it sounds strange, but I only now have an awareness that many do not enjoy the privileges I do. For me, the poor never really existed as my neighbor in the widest, best sense of the word. They existed in a background of my living an upper middle-class family life. As wonderful as economic success is (and we should go for it but not be controlled by it) it cannot be lawful and fulfilling if it is not shared. I love the give and take with the children, teens, and adults. I am the one with a sense of being enriched, just as I want to foster the enrichment of my new friends; we all have gifts, no matter our economic status. I receive love in giving it. My new brothers and sisters have given me a lot of love. Children are so great; we must protect them. I have the opportunity (it makes me feel alive) to be inspired by humble, courageous people. I finally get it: at heart there is no separation; we are the Mystical Body of Christ." Angelina tells me about the seven young girls and one six-year-old boy—all homeless—whom she lives with and cares for in Casa Matraca. Vanessa Torres describes going into the streets to support working children by providing snacks and supervising art projects. Octavio tells me about working against a newly proposed law that will lower the penal age of young people from 16 to 14 in the state of Veracruz.

That night, Easter Saturday, *Sábado de Gloria*, the packed cathedral, lights from orange-flamed candles passed to each other, spreading blessing rays to everyone, even to the bent-to-the-ground *anciana*, who is selling trinkets for pennies across the cobbled street. Yes, I think, better to pass on wishes to create happiness, rather than "to curse the darkness." Later, I say hi to two young sisters who sell and beg into the night. The older sister, age eight, recognizes me and takes my hand to see some laid out assorted bright-colored textiles with striking geometric shapes and artistically crafted images of birds, animals, humans, and flowers. She sways as a dancer in the dark, with red roses for sale in her arms. Her little sister, deep dark brown eyes expanded, listens to our conversation, quickly darting with an outreached hand to passers-by for a coin. Their vigilant mother is close by and comes over to greet me. She asks one of her boys to show me his juggling skills. Seems like all the family is engaged in making a living.

I am at Casa Matraca, a home for abandoned or needy children just outside the city. It was originally given to the Jesuits, and is now owned by Matraca, a civil work, incorporated as a non-profit organization without religious affiliation. Angelina lovingly takes care of the children and is called "Mom." Some of the children previously just lived on the streets where they were robbed, beaten, and sometimes forced into prostitution. Some lived in abusive families. Now they go to school and help in the house as well as receive medical attention and psychological counseling. Some will re-integrate with their families. In the evening, we have a birthday celebration for one of the girls. I see her crying because her mom who promised to come does not show up. "She never shows up." The children kiss her and sing Las Mañanitas to her and play the guitar and dance to Credence Clearwater and cumbias music. A party breaks out. It seems in our fun, at least for our few hours, we do not have a problem in the world.

Visiting families of Los Angeles students in the village of Miahuatlán, I am struck by the huge church hovering over the small homes, its dome at one end and a three-tiered bell tower at the other. Seems like mostly older folks and children remain, with young adults fleeing to the cities or to el sueño Americano. About two hundred of the population of the four thousand in town have made it across the border to join the 11,000,000 or so native-born Mexicans who live in the United States of America. Young people tell me they must leave because manufacturing, oil-producing, fishing, raising sugarcane, beans, bananas, coffee does not employ enough or pay enough. Some Compañeros have sent money for individual school tuitions (about $30 a year) and money for single moms with kids to buy puestos (about $40 for these small mobile stands to start a selling business). A fourteen-year-old girl who suffers from slight cerebral palsy runs one of the mobile stands. She is wearing a pink and white gauze dress and says hello; a customer asks her to demonstrate that a lighter she is selling works properly, but she just cannot quite manage. Spontaneously, seemingly out of nowhere, a swarthy young man sweeps the lighter out of her hand and elegantly flicks a flame to satisfy her nodding, approving customer.

Teaching English to Indigenous, and visiting them in Central America and Mexico—such colorful dress, so hospitable, seamless with Mother Nature—I was very much the student as well and came to embrace the extended meaning of "Chicano." I recall camping on cobblestone at the 1998 Congress for Indigenous, April 13–15 in Mexico City. Such an inspiring happening; so invigorated being there! Fifty-six different ethnic groups were represented, comingling and peacefully marching for *derechos humanos.* I lived with large groups on the packed *zócalo* (public square) for four days and three nights in tents, on this *gran plaza de México Viejo,* risen from *Lago de Texcoco,* consecrated land of Indian peoples. Watching were heavily armed soldiers who arrested some foreigners, so they could toss them out of the country. Indigenous people were tired of being submissive, exploited Indians, and demanded to be treated as equal human beings. There were marches and protests against economic oppression of Indian laborers and people. I heard various languages all around me: Tarahumara, Chol, Mixteco, Nahuatl, Zogue, Zapoteco. Banners flew, greens, reds, whites of the Mexican flag: *Dignidad para los Indigenos and Nunca mas un México sin Nosotros* (Dignity for the Indigenous and Never again a Mexico without Us). On the ruins of El Templo Mayor, the tall dusty crooked gray cathedral reflected light beams on the people, like reluctant blessings from a prudish grandmother. Inside the cathedral, I contemplated a painting of our Lady of Guadalupe and softly colored statues of Ignatius of Loyola, Philip Neri, Dominic; Francis Assisi faces a Black crucified Jesus, knees swayed and covered with a gold skirt.

Almost dawn, I was sleeping on blankets, sinking into this stone-blocked plaza, graced and warmed by friendly Indigenous, young and old, some speaking a little Spanish with me. Going to sleep, I envisioned golden Aztec temples, now finally enlightened, feathered priests dancing on tops of pyramids, supplicating Grace from the grand Mystery. In my reverie, we, though I was a foreigner, were together, calling for a brand new—and non-violent—kind of human sacrifice to each other.

I was so enriched and nourished by my time with people and families of Southern Mexico: *tristezas*, *alegrías*, sharing ideas, hugs, laughter and crying, the sudden sweetness of children.

6

Reflecting on Forgiveness

True forgiveness can only arise organically, after a genuine healing process. Only then is it authentic. Forgiveness is one of the primary mantras preached by the New Cage and "Positive Psychology" movements. They often encourage people to forgive independent of extensive emotional processes, as though forgiveness is merely a thought, or a concept, or something that can be willed. Some even go so far as to suggest that you must always heal your wounds directly with the wrongdoers and remain connected to them. Putting our focus on forgiving a wrongdoer before we have prioritized working through our anger and pain, is another way we imprison consciousness and overturn reasonable principles of accountability. Yes, forgiveness can be a beautiful thing, but it is essential that it arises authentically. Forgiveness is not the first place to go after an abusive relationship or a traumatic experience. Healing is.
—Jeff Brown

Many years ago, one of my students came to class with a fresh black eye she could not hide. Luckily, a counselor was nearby and took the student to her office to ascertain whether she was in danger. Later the counselor told me the student's coming to class was a cry for help against her abusive boyfriend who would sometimes punch her in the face and stomach when arguing. "Do I have to forgive him again and take him back?" "I'm frightened for my life." The counselor urged her to get to safety and to heal

81

herself before talking forgiveness which, despite the pleas of the boyfriend, had not worked in the past. The attentive counselor arranged for her to stay with her mother and father who were welcoming to their daughter, and eventually she obtained a restraining order. About five months later, she came back to class. She looked happy, with free energy to concentrate on one of her important goals: to learn English.

Forgiveness, not meaning condoning, generally is based on the willingness to let go of "getting even" with our tormenter, but are there times to get even, to pay back a wrong? Or can I at least wish my abuser harm to make up for grave harm inflicted on me? After all, forgiveness cannot be forced, cannot be pretended if it is to be real. Certainly, we should forgive ourselves and each other for the everyday mistakes and moments of meanness, stupidity, and impatience we all experience. Sometimes we do not treat ourselves and others well; we are human beings. I've met some couples who say, "It's really helpful for us not to go to bed angry, or at least not for an extended period of time, to let go of offenses that we seem to exaggerate, but which we don't have to dwell on for an excessive amount of time. We say 'sorry' and accept sincere apologies; we laugh and relax."

Twenty years ago, I visited Julio, a cousin of one of my students. Julio told me he both paid-back/got-even and forgave at the same time. He lived in a small farming community in the state of Veracruz, Mexico, where there was no law enforcement for miles. Drinking beers as the sun slowly fell to sleep on the pink horizon, he told me his sister had been a victim of an attempted rape by her classmate. She got away but showed up at home, bruised, bloody, hysterical, only calming down for a few seconds to name her attacker. Julio at that very moment went on horseback with his brother, armed with iron bars to punish the offender. With a tender face and voice, Julio said, "We had a responsibility to our sister, Gertrudis, and to our society. We pummeled her abuser; we broke bones and were done with it. We did not curse him to hell, but asked God to forgive him as he forgives us all. Our forgiveness was saying *enough* punishment (just punishment was delivered) and not having the hateful intention of wishing him eternal condemnation or that bad things happen to him in this life."

"Forgiving means that we choose to release resentment, hatred, bitterness, desires for revenge for wrongs done to us; it is a way to come to peace with the past. In forgiving, we decide to break our troubling connection to the offender. We realize that no offense is worth the price of destroying our peace. Forgiving is taking the arrows out of our gut, rather than twisting them around inside us. We move away from it beyond the offender and the offense and take full responsibility for our present happiness. We choose to forgive so that we will suffer less and be free to live. Forgiving is a personal choice that does not depend on the offender's deserving it, asking for it, or expressing remorse—although this certainly can make forgiving easier. Forgiving is about the offended person's inner strength, rather than the offender's offense. We voluntarily forgive because we realize that getting even does not heal." (*The Anger Management Sourcebook*, Schiraldi and Kerr, p.182)

****

I am impressed with the way Olivia Porter (TEDx Chicago, June 18, 2019) insightfully presents on YouTube, "Forget Forgiveness and Harness Hate." An engaging Olivia reflects on her experience helping abused women in a shelter to learn job interview skills. She queries if the audience have ever heard the unexamined, unnuanced, simplistic clichés: "There's no love without forgiveness." "There's no peace without forgiveness." "Forgiveness is a gift you give yourself." The majority raised their hands. Olivia affirms the importance of forgiving, not holding grudges for "the small stuff." Stuff not worth sweating, which most is. But what about one of Olivia's students in the shelter, whose abusive boyfriend molested her daughter, used her money which she had saved for her education, and put her in the hospital? Should she forgive right away, as many were coaxing her to do, prods Olivia, or should she hate, using its emotional energy to mobilize the natural healing of the body-mind-heart?

"Hate is an intense or passionate dislike for someone, a strong aversion to something." I hate cancer because it took the lives of my parents. "I hate my current circumstance of being in an abusive relationship." Olivia distinguishes hate from violent anger. Anger, we lash out, are reactive; hate, we are proactive. The University College London did a study in which people's brains were mapped as they viewed a picture of someone they detested. Hate activated the parts of the brain controlling movement and the frontal cortex controlling reasoning and critical thinking. Hmmm, movement and reasoning, could this be a winning combination, free flowing energy matched with an ability to make reasonable (have a chance to succeed) plans in one's own best interests?

Olivia's student was being rushed into forgiving her boyfriend. She was asked to write repetitiously, "I forgive . . ." (writing name of her torturer over and over). Olivia said, "Instead, why not write what you hate, and then turn it to love and your own happiness?"

Sure, I can do that: I hate that he molested my daughter; I hate that he took my money, my chance to invest in education; and I hate that he devastatingly put me in the hospital.

Thank you. Okay, prompts Olivia, add *love* to your sentences.

I hate that he molested my daughter because I love my daughter. I hate that he stole my money because I love education. I hate that he put me in the hospital because I love my health.

"Hate makes Love obvious. Hate protects against threats to loved ones."

Now, my Sister, write about what you love. How does it make you feel to write with a focus on love? Will you naturally go past hate, use it still but with more emphasis on a growing, healing love? Perhaps this will put you in the right frame of mind to decide whether you forgive or not?

I love my daughter, I love my education, I love my good health. Yes, I can write that several times, magnifying love's shine in my heart. O that feels so good to let Love sink in! Love in all its flavors is the juice of Life.

My health improves, I am happier and able to go with energy and direction, for dreams for me, my daughter, my learning, my well-being.

✶✶✶✶✶✶✶✶

On December 19, 2008, the unimaginable happened to Sarah Montana. (TEDx Lincoln Square, 2018, "The Real Risk of Forgiveness—and Why It's Worth It") How do you cope with the murder of one's mother and brother by a 17-year-old boy, a friend's brother whom Sarah barely knew? The boy had previously broken into her family's home to raid their snack cabinet. The mother said: "He's going through a hard time." But appallingly the boy broke into their home a last time looking for things to sell for cash. He panicked when he came across Sarah's brother, Jim, sleeping on the sofa and shot Jim to death. Realizing he had forgotten his coat, he returned to the home, and finding the mother screaming uncontrollably, also shot her because she recognized him. The young adolescent was sentenced to two back-to-back life sentences and locked up in a prison in southwest Virginia. Sara commemorates her beloved mother, "Mama" to all the children and teens in the community. Mama often left her front door unlocked and her snack cabinet full. She'd tell kids she ran into: "I see you. I know you and I love you Sky Big." "Mother's wholeness," Sarah said, "was the sun, and kids just gravitated toward it. Even when I can't feel it or see it—the sun of my wholeness may be covered in clouds—it is never gone."

In the summer of 2016, Sarah Montana quit her job to write a play about the murder of her mother and brother. She told people her play was about art, but in truth Sarah was on a "vision quest" for closure. For seven years, she had said she forgave the perpetrator of the heinous violation of her family but realized that saying it did not mean she was doing it. She thought that forgiveness was the right thing to do but became aware there is no timeline for forgiveness. She felt the pressure from others for her to forgive, but she realized that pleasing others did not consider the personal process necessary for forgiving the double murder of her mother and brother. A quick forgiveness would only relieve her friends' discomfort around her, but would not mean that she was healed. She had to face anger, grief, and trauma.

Sarah decided to use Google to find out about the young man imprisoned for his evil deeds. She found out that the man was likely in solitary confinement 23 hours a day in an 8' x 10' cell. The prison had been criticized for "case after case" of human rights violations; there was a hunger strike at the prison in 2012. To Sarah, unexpectedly, the young man became a person, not the face of all evil. "I imagined him crying out from his cell. I don't want to hold us captive anymore."

So why forgive? "So that I can be set free. I look at my wounds, face what happened to me, so I know what I'm forgiving." Sarah wrote the imprisoned young man a letter. "What you did to me is not OK. But you do not owe me anything. I cannot be reduced to this one event. To be whole, I wish you a lifetime of healing." Kind wishes in place of curses. Sarah had healed enough to mean what she wrote in her letter. She could let go of her pain, grief, and anger which were part of her healing. Even her anger, short of violence, had been a fire, "which cauterized her wounds." Letting go of expectations, she was able to finally forgive, reclaiming herself. She had chosen "to keep us connected," but now she wanted to be liberated from him. Forgiveness was "the only way to get rid of this dude; it was like breaking free from a blood oath chaining our story with his forever." Sarah said she chose herself while not consigning the young man to simply the role of a villain, making "evil the sum of his parts." She experienced the freedom she longed for.

Let's continue our conversation with Sarah Montana in "What Shapes You, Can't Break You, " YouTube, October 30, 2019. "When a high school boyfriend took my virginity without asking me first, I went a little crazy. Did I break up with him? No, of course not. I did backflips of logic to convince myself that I loved him because I had to stay close to my pieces." Sarah remained with her boyfriend for three years, "withering away in silent shame, all the way down to 90 lbs." Finally, she opened up to her 17-year-old brother Jim and best friend Joe. Both said she must leave her boyfriend and *now!* "It never occurred to me that I could do that." Three hours later her brother saw her curled up in a ball, heaving, sobbing.

"How did I let this happen? I must be a bad person. I am so broken." But Jim would have nothing to do with her self-blaming, and he "scooped me up like a baby and rocked me." Jim then sat Sarah up. Holding her shoulders and looking into her eyes: "Now you stop that. You are beautiful. You've saved my life every day. Anything you say bad about yourself cuts into me as if you said it about me. Stop crying and I'm going to make you the best sandwich you've ever had in your life." Her brother didn't see her "pieces," he saw "all of me." Sarah could feel her brother's appreciative love, his recognition that she was, at the core, an exceptionally good person: "Even though I was covered with bruises, my brother didn't think I should be thrown away like a bad piece of fruit. I am not my pieces, there are no pieces of me. I cannot be broken. I can be bruised, dented sure, but I am always whole." Sarah praised a writing teacher who also pointed out to her that she in essence is whole, bigger than the role she plays, not confined to pieces. Her teacher's first assignment was to answer three questions. Who Are You? What Has Shaped You? What Do you Want to Be?

****

"I'm never going to forgive that degraded, sick bastard who raped me. He's not a human being, I wish he were dead," my friend told me some months after she had been raped by an acquaintance. However, three years later she was able to forgive in her own way. I wondered how she navigated a difficult path of letting go of revenge. How was my friend finally able to forgive the man who violated her? Diogenes wrote: "Forgiveness is better than revenge." But it's not so easy, she told me, to let go of person-hating (the *act is* always hated) which is forgiving. "I'm not forgetting; I'm not being goody-goody. I'm giving up wanting to hurt back. I meditate, as well as talk to the counselor, so I can truly observe the feelings going on within me. If there are still suppressed feelings, my forgiveness isn't integrated into my personality." It's *not* a quick process to forgive if you've been raped, she emphasized. It's a terrible trauma, a violation of your sacred space and dignity. But my friend realized, as did Sarah, that she could be bruised, dented, violated, but that she was "always whole." Going to pieces without falling apart. Erin Prizzey says so poignantly: "I have been raped. It pollutes one's life. It is an experience that is contained within the boundaries of one's own life. In the end, one's life is larger. Assault by a stranger or within a relationship is very terrible. One is hurt, undermined, degraded, afraid. But one's life is larger."

✶✶✶✶✶✶✶✶

I would like to re-tell a story which involves physical trauma, its healing, and its lessons of forgiveness based on human interconnectedness. First there was letting go any plan for revenge and then with time a spiritual, blessing forgiveness because I sensed at least at moments, that I have some connection to my violent assailants, even though it may be a tiny thread between us. I ceased wishing my attackers bad vibrations. I wanted to stand completely apart but it became impossible. So, I quietly bless family, friends, blessing all, giving up cursing those who may have hurt me (even though I may not want anything to do with them).

On a black cold night, I looked up at the moon, 238,900 miles away but still touchable, bright, and present shining. Taking a deep breath, I felt I could swim with distant stars and launch myself through limitless skies into a universe stretching 13.8 billion years, all Being, afar and intimate, distant horizons vibrating within me, an infinity of causes and effects, continually evolving, inter-acting, exploding, giving birth, subsisting, dying, recycling, and transforming. Closely related in a luminescent, mysterious process, beyond our capacity to fully know, our existence brings us joys as well as disasters we cannot fathom or control. Extreme, shocking, and traumatizing events can awaken us from our daily routine and arouse a new and dramatic perspective. We are interdependent and connected to everything and everyone, even to that which is abhorrent—the most violent and hostile of our species. That which is in all people is likewise to some extent in me. I am a tiny participant, along with you, in this cosmic dancing with the stars.

Soon after I exited a 7-Eleven in Hollywood (how mad I later would be at myself for stopping to get orange juice on the way to visiting my sister Mary), just before dark, six enraged assailants attacked, four making a circle to hide two gangbangers throwing punches and landing kicks. The police would later say I resembled an older version of a rival gang member, *hombre alto*, "tall man." They did not go for my wallet. Full of vengeance, their objective was to kill me. I fought back as best I could. For a couple of years in the early 1980s, I learned basic Taekwondo at Master Chun Lee's studio on Rosemead Boulevard, across from the Southeast Asian Refugee program, run by El Monte-Rosemead Adult School. Master Lee taught us Korean martial arts self-defense: kicks, punches, footwork, a series of moves, attacking, and warding off blows. And to be aware of our environment, our breath, and posture. Despite that training, the end—

though delayed a few moments—came quickly. I was punched, head-butted, and finally one of them broke from the circle and plunged a long pearl-gray blade deep into my stomach, severing my renal vein and slicing my left kidney in half. Blood gushed from the wound. I credit Master Lee for his instruction. I was able to summon reflexive techniques to mitigate the effects of the vicious stabbing. When I stop by to say hi to Chun Lee, I feel gratitude, and chagrin that I did not continue practicing Taekwondo.

The thugs disappeared into a surreal twilight zone between life and death. I experienced the thin line separating passing out and somehow willfully hanging onto consciousness. For a few seconds of expansive awareness, a part of me rose into the sky and calmly floated above my body, a crumbling, bleeding mess. I pressed the wound in my stomach to stop the massive blood flow. Doctors later told me that, by putting pressure on my wound, I was the first in a team to save my life. To live, I needed to be saved by a Good Samaritan. Frightened passersby rushed from the desperate scene. Cars slowed and then screeched away, ignoring my pleas for help. A few drivers stopped, opened their doors, changed their minds and fled. For perhaps fifteen minutes, I held my wound as tightly as I could, telling myself to breathe, keep awake and not give in to the overwhelming sensation to faint. If I pass out, I joked, I will die near a 7-Eleven, instead of in front of Grauman's Chinese Theater in Hollywood. Not this way! Not murdered by Hispanics, so many of whom I love.

Unafraid, my Good Samaritan, Mike Bunnel—an avid Christian I would later learn—stopped, opened, but did not shut, his car door. He took me to the emergency room at Kaiser Hospital on Sunset Boulevard, just a few blocks from where I was stabbed. I was in for a long surgery to repair the sliced renal vein and left kidney—my recovery would be slow, one step at a time. It's a mystery that such an unwanted event led to my sensing the inter-connectedness of the at- tackers, a hero who saved my life, the surgeons-nurses-therapists who healed me, police, friends, students, and family visiting me in the hospital: all coming together. This unexpected, difficult trauma angered me at times, but with time, mostly I felt grateful to be alive and willing to forgive. As police showed me pictures of gang members, I noticed their resemblance to some of my students: dark, Latin, handsome, looking older, more hardened than their ages. You hurt me, *her- manos*, but, though it has taken time, I truly forgive you. I cannot like you, but I will not close my heart to you, sending you blessings rather than curses. I agree to cooperate with the police to find you, young men, who perpetrated a pay- back on the "wrong man." You need to face the conse- quences of your harmful actions. I could identify two of the six gang members, but the police gave up after a year of searching. No witnesses came forward.

I would later visit the doctors, therapists, and nurses to thank them and give small gifts. A female therapist at Kaiser once asked, "Do you want to talk about it?" I just wept the entire hour with her; her warm, open, and understanding presence unearthed deeply buried tears. Without Mike's generosity, good luck, and the preparedness of expert med- ical care, I would not have survived.

On five occasions I spoke with police officers who visited during my hospitalization. They related that a different gang in the same week had stabbed an elderly man in the spine, taking his wallet and watch, the cruel act paralyzing him from the waist down. Police expressed frustration with the huge gang problem in Los Angeles. We talked about the gangs from El Salvador, Mexico, Vietnam, East and South

LA. I told them about my Vietnamese, Salvadoran, and Mexican students, and that I had attended funerals for some of them, who were murdered in drive-by shootings. We lamented the senseless loss of young people. I sadly remembered two untimely deaths at a facility in Baldwin Park where I taught: Francisco, a bright, promising, charismatic resident, former gang member, was found dead in the bathroom, a needle stuck in his vein for a heroin fix; and Lewis, a tall, thin, handsome Vietnam veteran who was discovered one early gray morning hanging dead from a tree in the yard. Lewis was soft spoken and gentle, but haunted by the emotional, conscious and unconscious memories of war, "death's feast."

At times, our hospital/police business conversations wandered into our personal lives. I had never felt close to police officers, nor had I thought much about how tough their jobs were, in often hostile surroundings. Here we were, officer and victim, interviewer and interviewee, engaged in police business yet also enjoying ourselves in our varied conversations, some humorous. At times, laughter hurt my stapled stomach. Sometimes I was groaning in pain from the after-effects of a long surgical wound, zippered together from my stomach to the bottom of my chest. Violence in my attackers, kindness of an ordinary hero, dedicated nurses and doctors, encouragement, thoughtfulness, connecting with caring police officers. All in all, I was a lucky man.

✶✶✶✶✶✶✶✶

Consuming 40,000,000 tons of material per second to sustain us, the Sun is exploding as one of four hundred billion stars in the Milky Way, swimming in the cosmic sea of 100 billion galaxies. We are small, yet of great value, with a precious opportunity to live our lives, in harmony and purpose with the stars, moon, sun and Earth intermingling, the whole vibrating mesh of life coursing through us in every breath.

7

Alice's Notorious Baby Farm

The shortage of adoptable babies has created a system in which everyone in the triad is vulnerable to exploitation. I want to state my bias clearly: the needs of the child must be put before those of the birth parents, the adoptive parents and the legal agents involved. The child must be seen as a real person—not a fantasy child, not an idealized child, not a special child, not a commodity—but a child with his own genetics, his own talents, and his own identity, a child allowed to grow up in an open environment without secrets about who she is or where she comes from, a child with two sets of parents that gave him a dual identity. The best interests of the child are in the best interests of the adoptive family, the birth family, and society.
—Betty Jean Lifton

During the first three years of a child's life, her experiences have a tremendous effect on how she will view herself and others, how she will act or behave, how she will respond emotionally and, perhaps, physically to events and relationships, and the kinds of generalizations she forms from her experiences. Given the importance of this neurological phenomenon, it is a bit disconcerting that much of the memory we have of this time is implicit memory: experiences that greatly influence our responses to the world and those in it, but that we cannot recall.
—Nancy Verrier

I researched Alice R. P. Satterthwaite, who arranged my adoption and was arrested for baby trafficking. Satterthwaite was accused of operating a nation-wide black-market adoption racket: "brazen bedside solicitation of unwanted babies of both unmarried and married mothers." A March 8, 1949 *Lubbock Avalanche Journal* headline read: "Former Social Worker Charged with Operation of Baby Farm." Alice provided pre-natal care, obstetrical services, and most coveted secrecy in exchange for the right to have the baby adopted for a high price.

Alice Satterthwaite was a hard-nosed child trafficker who, through an illegal adoption agency, sold babies, bypassing the legal adoption system. She made money from my procurement by my adoptive parents. She sold me. My biological mother decided (I am sure with good intentions) instead of giving me to my Black family, to have me adopted by a White family which would most likely be more privileged than a Black family. I totally regret not being placed with my father and his Black Haitian family but understand the taboos of the times. This does not negate my appreciation for my adoptive parents, Morgan and Helen Callahan. But in my bones, only talking for me, I sense blood (my basic identity) is thicker than water (my adoptive identity). That is why I would have chosen, if I had any say, to be raised by my Haitian family.

I have come to feel that the racial tension in our society and history, with an impulse to right-calm-transform it, is in a small but meaningful way literally in the blood that flows in my veins. John Lewis, may he enjoy Eternal Light and Happiness, reminds us: "In 1956 I was only 16 years old; we went to the public library and were told by the librarian that the library was for whites only! Segregation and racial discrimination were not in keeping with our faith, so we had to do something. . . . You have to take that long hard look and just believe that if you are consistent, you will succeed." In memory of John Lewis for his charismatic leadership, together we can take our own present-day, long hard look at our society, commit ourselves to social justice and responsibility, consistently giving energy to overcoming racial discrimination against any race. Since the pandemic outbreak in March 2020, there has been an alarming increase of violent racist assaults and robberies of Asians. If we take care of and know ourselves, if we are tolerant, and stick together, with persistence and patience, we will succeed to the delight of the prophetic John Lewis still motivating us from Heaven.

****

Baby-selling was prevalent in NYC and other cities in the United States after the World War II baby boom. Families wanted babies and since there were not enough through legal adoption, they turned to baby brokers operating clandestinely outside the law. "Babies were not cheap and baby-selling proved to be such a lucrative business that New York authorities uncovered a million-dollar adoption scheme in 1959 that included loan-sharking and gambling. The price of babies discussed during the Kefauver hearings related to black market adoptions ranged from $1,500 to $5,000 or more. The median family income in 1956 was $4,800; clearly the trade involved a wealthy clientele. The expense reflected the many middlemen and women involved. Birth mothers received stipends, maternity home operators were reimbursed for room and board for the women waiting to give birth, doctors received money for deliveries, lawyers got paid arranging the adoptions, and sometimes judges received payoffs for approving the adoptions." ("The Shameful Practice of Buying and Selling Babies Doesn't Only Happen Overseas, but Here in the US, too", History News

Network, George Washington University, Janet Golden,
May 13, 2018)

Kraft Television Theater, influenced by the 1955
Kefauver hearings, in 1956 presented the melodrama, "Babies for Sale." A prospective father haggles with a baby broker who brags, "I understand you want our merchandise but
do not want to pay our price, but I'm doing business in a
seller's market." It is the story of a couple, desperate to have
an infant because the mother lost her child at birth. Wanting
to avoid the long, tedious legal route to adopting, the couple
turns to the black market to adopt a replacement child. They
are shown babies and become particularly attached to one,
whose baby's nurse complicates matters by urging the couple to adopt legally to be sure the best interests of the child
would be kept foremost in mind.

Alice Satterthwaite pleaded guilty to a lesser charge of
not having a license to get all the other charges dropped. She
was allowed to plead out to the lesser charge because she was
prepared to drag into the trial the US Army and the
American Red Cross, which she alleged sought her services
when Army nurses became pregnant during WWII.
Obviously, these allegations would have been very
embarrassing to the Army and the Red Cross. Hundreds of
adoptive parents, as well as birth mothers, were terrified that
their adoptions would be exposed in the investigation.
Evidently, according to the news reports, one birth mother
had gone so far as to threaten suicide over the fear that she
would be "outed"! It was clear from the news reports that
Alice was indeed running a "baby mill" and that she made
some unbelievably bad placements. She appears to have
gotten off with a slap on the wrist in large part because she
had influential friends and many scared clients.

My mother must have faced exceedingly difficult and complicated challenges, endured at a NYC maternity home where the mothers were pressured to give up their babies for adoption. They would be threatened with bills for room, board, and medical expenses if the mother kept her baby. I love and respect my mother because she cared for me *in utero* and for three years, which was for the times uncommon. I imagine her in a city maternity home, lonely, ashamed, conflicted, determined to face with the best of her ability giving birth to her son. Going back in circular time, I send her blessings of Light, of appreciation and comfort that no matter what happens we, mother and son, are always together.

With insight and compassion, Martine, a mom herself, empathized with my mother: "The decision to give you up must not have been an easy one for your biological mother. Times were very different back then. I know you have forgiven her, and that all you have now from her is the love that she felt for you during that time she got to know you. I'm sure that it's that same love that she remembered and kept in heart her whole life. Keeping her precious secret for her alone. It's the one thing she and you shared, somewhat of a complicity, a tight two-person circle."

With the benefit of a host of new research and discoveries, I was able to discern four key events that took place in rapid succession in 1947 that, taken together, would shape my life forever. My mother left me in her grandfather's home in Massachusetts to be raised in the safety, care, and comfort of her mother, grandfather, and her brother and his wife. Mother was living and working in Washington, DC, and France. In May 1947, she made an emergency return home from France after receiving word that her beloved grandfather was dying. Unbeknownst to her or her family, when she arrived, she was not alone. She was a few weeks pregnant with my half-brother. Her grandfather, my great-grandfather, was the venerable family patriarch, an eminent surgeon, who, before the war, had been the highly respected Chief of Surgery at a hospital in Paris. Sadly, he died on May 27, 1947. May he enjoy the Eternal Love of God.

Throughout my great-grandfather's life, he openly and willingly offered his care and protection to those in need—even when it was at great risk to himself. A telling incident occurred in 1908, when he was arrested, and ultimately expelled from Odessa, Russia, for revolutionary activities. A well authenticated example is that, "though not a Jew . . . during the pogroms there he had harbored a number of Jewish refugees in his house and been otherwise sympathetically active in their cause." (*The American Jewish Yearbook of the American Jewish Committee*: September 16, 1909 to October 3, 1910.) With my unending gratitude, I acknowledge his protective care. I, his illegitimate mixed-race great-grandchild, was given not only his name, but also his home, where I was sheltered and raised for the first—so vital—three years of my life. Child-development research convincingly affirms that the first three years of life are the most critical in shaping a child's brain, learning skills, and social and emotional abilities. Alice withheld all information about my first three years from my adoptive parents, the courts, and me, and falsely attested that my birth father was dead at the time of my birth. Because of my successful search, I discovered where and how I spent those crucial years, and the important role my great-grandfather played in providing me a loving, stable home.

Merci, mon cher arrière-grand-père!

Upon my great-grandfather's death I would quickly lose all of his gifts: my name, my home, my native language, and his protection. I also soon lost the rest of my maternal family. Expecting a baby, my mother married the father, and together they returned to France where her second son was born. My mother left me in the care of her mother and brother and his wife back in Massachusetts. Then my mother reestablished contact with Alice Satterthwaite, the child trafficker. Without my great-grandfather there to object, I was quietly handed over to Alice on November 19, 1947, the day before my third birthday.

"Nothing is known of this child's life up to this date."

✱✱✱✱✱✱✱✱

I've written glowingly about my Haitian family's acceptance of me, but it's a different story with my mother's family. I reached out to relatives on my mother's side (names withheld out of consideration for their privacy) to see if they would like to meet. I was intrigued and enthused to possibly have the chance to connect with blood relatives on my mother's side. They would perhaps also be as interested in knowing me as I was in getting to know them. I anticipated hearing stories about my mother. Taking a few deep breaths, I wrote a letter to two of my half-siblings, saying that I would like to connect with them, but that, of course, it was up to them. They did not answer my letter of self-introduction, which included my original birth certificate and adoption papers. Most likely they had no idea about me, and it was disturbing to them that their mom had a secret love child so many years ago. What for me in my feeling imagination was an intense romantic love affair of the two high-powered people who gave me life was for them, I surmise, a shameful occurrence, as "illegitimacy" was considered in the 1940s and 1950s. What for me was a relationship, however short, to be celebrated was for them an occurrence to be kept hidden. I respect their decision not to meet me, with well wishes, naturally, going out to them.

Alice Satterthwaite heaped mounds of deceit on my roots. But through a long and grace-filled process, I finally uncovered them, embodying, integrating my four parents who together are the principal influencers of my whole self. I feel an emotional and spiritual appreciative awareness of each of them every day. It has been especially vital to me to understand Mother's times.

"Out of innocent confusion . . . was born heartbreak," begins the trailer for the 1949 film, *Not Wanted*, aka *Shame*, directed and produced by Hollywood star Ida Lupino and co-produced by Elmer Clifton. It portrays an unmarried, pregnant mother, who lived in the time of my beloved biological mother when out-of-wedlock pregnancy was stigmatized. My mother was pressured by strong social prejudice, which prevailed until the 1960s against unmarried mothers and their "illegitimate," "bastard" offspring (even more so if bi-racial). "Illegitimate" designated unmarried mothers, unmarried fathers, and their children as "deviants," and "outcasts," legally and socially inferior to "legitimate" members of a family based in a married couple.

"Before the 1960s, unmarried mothers were usually considered undeserving of the public benefits offered to impoverished widows and deserted wives. They were generally denied mothers' pensions, which virtually all states granted beginning in 1910, and Aid to Dependent Children, a federal program created by the Social Security Act of 1935. Divorced women and non-White women were also excluded. To be illegitimate was to be shamed and shunned. Those who lived under the shadow of illegitimacy were endangered. They needed help, according to reformers and policymakers, who insisted that alleviating the stigma associated with illegitimate birth status would do more to improve child welfare and family life than either contempt or condemnation." So, it is understandable, though terribly sad, that my biological mother and her family wanted my birth and the first three years of my life erased. My original birth certificate was sealed. A new, amended certificate was issued, under the name "Morgan Callahan," claiming that my adoptive parents were my birth parents. None of this was true. (Cf. the outstanding Adoption History Project, University of Oregon, https://pages.uoregon.edu/adoption/)

In 1948, there is the first recorded transracial adoption of an African American child by a White couple. New York State, in 1949, would outlaw black-market child trafficking but the law was unenforceable. From 1953–1958, the National Urban League Foster Care and Adoption Project nationally coordinated an effort to locate homes for African American children. In 1953, Jean Paton (1908–2002), a pioneering reformer, founded Orphan Village, the first adoptee search and support network. In her 1954 book, *The Adopted Break Silence* (Philadelphia: Life History Study Center), she provides a forum for adoptees to tell their stories (positive, negative, and mixed), proffering adoptees a sense of distinct identity, that adoption—among other human institutions—"is a process which influences an individual life for many years beyond its initiation." By the time she began collecting the forty life stories that appeared in *The Adopted Break Silence*, most states in the country had instituted policies of confidentiality and sealed records, making search and reunion a virtual impossibility. Paton spent her adult life seeking to overturn adoption secrecy and frequently took positions well in advance of her contemporaries. She suggested the creation of a mutual consent registry as early as 1949, for example, and embraced the term "bastard" in the 1970s, declaring "Bastards Are Beautiful" long before the era of Bastard Nation. "Let them look away from their paralyzing silences and their secrets and see whether speech has something to offer them." (Adoption History Project, University of Oregon)

Marley Greiner is the Executive Chair and co-founder of the provocatively named Bastard Nation, the Adoptee Rights Organization, which is the largest adoptee civil rights organization in the US. She has testified before many state legislatures in the support of the right of adoptees to access their original birth certificate (OBC). It has usually been the intent of adoption agencies to serve the best interests of the child being adopted, but in earlier years this "serving of the best interests of the child" caved in to "hiding the child's illegitimate birth from the public" even if it meant depriving the child's birth identity, not allowing the child (should he or she want it) full access to information of heritage.

****

Thanks to the Heavens, I was spared from the most notorious child trafficker of all, Georgia Tann (1891–1950), deceitful, apparently psychotic Memphis social worker, who stole an estimated five thousand children, 19 of whom died from abuse. Tann started children trafficking in 1924 with 80% of the children going to New York and California. Through pressure tactics, false pretenses, and threats of legal action, she would coerce mostly single poor mothers to give up their children. She stole babies to sell them, some from loving homes or from maternity wards of hospitals, some through duping the fearful mother to give up the baby on her own. She had judges, social workers, and lawyers (some of whom she provided with babies) in her pocket. She was protected greatly by the shady former Memphis mayor and political boss, E. H. Crump, and by corrupt Family Court Judge Camille Kelley. Georgia Tann helped standardize the sealing of original birth certificates and issuing amended ones in which the adopted parents are listed as the original mother and father, birth child and mother-father relationship legally hidden away. Scouts would especially be on the lookout for blond blue-eyed children from parents with little resources to pursue a stolen child. But what anguish they must have felt losing their babies to greedy Georgia Tann!

Tann would send two of her female employees, four to six babies in tow, to New York and California every three weeks. They would stay in hotels and meet with wealthy prospective parents who would pay $700 for a baby. Using an inflation calculator, that was $12,955.05 in today's money. Joan Crawford and June Allyson/Dick Powell were famous customers. Tann used the unlicensed home, the Tennessee Children's Home, "as a front for her black-market baby adoption scheme from the 1920s, until a state investigation into numerous instances of adoption fraud being perpetrated by her closed the institution in 1950. Tann died of cancer before the investigation made its findings public. While in her care, Tann mistreated the children, with reports of neglect, physical and sexual abuse, and murder." (Wikipedia)

For a can't-put-it-down, disturbing, compelling book, you can get the full story from *The Baby Thief: The Untold Story of Georgia Tann, the Baby Seller Who Corrupted Adoption* by Barbara Bisantz Raymond.

Ann Fessler, author of the illuminating book, *The Girls Who Went Away: The Hidden History of Women Who*

Surrendered Children for Adoption in the Decades Before Roe v. Wade, kindly emailed me after reading my account of Lionel Durand in *The Haitian Times*.

"Thanks for sending me a link to your story. It is fascinating! How *incredible* to discover you had such an amazing father! I am sure it brings you a lot of joy and pride. I hope the stories in my book bring you some peace and a fuller understanding of the pressures on unmarried women at that time. Having a bi-racial child would have made things even more difficult for your mother. I interviewed several women (both White and Black) who had bi-racial children in the 1960s and it was tough for them then, 20 years later."

A Swedish proverb says that sorrow shared is halved, and joy shared is doubled. Alice brought me (and other children) sorrow, but in sharing, it doesn't sting so much. In the next chapter about a wise mentor, my joy will be doubled.

8

A Spirituality of Adoption

A human being is a part of the whole called by us "the universe," a part limited in time and space. He experiences himself, his thoughts and feelings as something separate from the rest—a kind of optical delusion of his consciousness. This delusion is a kind of prison for us, restricting us to our personal desires and affection for a few persons nearest us. Our task must be to free ourselves from this prison by widening our circle of understanding and compassion to embrace all living creatures and the whole of nature in its beauty.
—Albert Einstein

The task of an authentic spirituality of adoption is to overcome the dualism that pits body against soul, matter against spirit, nature against nurture, and to embrace the truth, that we as adopted persons are not disembodied ghosts but embodied spirits who have received the gift of self from four separate individuals.
—Father Thomas F. Brosnan

We cannot separate action for justice from the proclamation of the Word of God.
—Fr. Pedro Arrupe, SJ, Jesuit Superior General 1965–1983

Grounded in the Gospel and Catholic social teaching, the Society of Jesus, in 1965, strengthened and placed at the center of its mission a commitment to "the service of faith and the promotion of justice." This

priority, a faith that does justice, links the authentic following of the Gospel of Jesus with an obligation to address the
social realities of poverty, oppression, and injustice in our
world.

Robert Mills Holstein Jr. (born November 3, 1941) was
a personal-injury lawyer who poured much of his time, and
his considerable earnings, into living a life as a man for others, a compassionate advocate for human rights and social
justice. On January 5, 2003, he died of pneumonia in the
arms of his devoted wife, Loretta, at a Riverside, California,
hospital. May our dear Compañero, Holy Rascal, enjoy Eternal Light. Bob studied from 1960 to 1967 to be a Jesuit priest
and left the Order some five years short of ordination. Even
after leaving, Bob felt he was still a Jesuit at heart. In the early
1980s he organized an annual reunion of former and current
Jesuits. These reunions became an incubator for a series of
social justice projects, and the informal group gradually
evolved into a more formal organization. In 1998, Bob
founded the West Coast Companeros, Inc. a 501(c)(3) with
the mission of supporting and challenging the Society of Jesus in its own aim to live a faith that does justice, in both its
educational work and helping poor and marginalized people
build better lives. WCCI continues as a band of former Jesuits and their life-partners, along with some active members
of the Society of Jesus.

In 1997, Bob and Loretta visited Jesuit Superior General,
Father Peter-Hans Kolvenbach, SJ, in Rome. Bob told the
following story: "I emailed Fr. Kolvenbach, telling him I was
going to be in Rome, and he invited me to come see him. We
had a great visit. I told him I was coming to share with him
some of the ideas our guys have, and how we're getting involved in different work. I mentioned to him that many feel
like they are as much a Jesuit as they ever were when they

were in the Society. Father Kolvenbach told me: 'I think they are Jesuits. Although it's not necessarily true canonically, I would say they are Jesuits.'" At the funeral Mass for Bob, Rev. John Baumann, SJ, gave a homily to a standing-room-only crowd of more than a thousand at the Riverside Convention Center. "Holstein just considered himself a Jesuit who was a little ahead of his time. He was passionate about justice and fairness for all peoples, particularly the poor and disenfranchised."

Bob spent years organizing annual November demonstrations at the gate of the US Army base at Ft. Benning, Georgia, protesting the agenda of the Army's School of the Americas (Western Hemisphere Institute for Security Cooperation), a training ground for Latin American military officers. Some of these soldiers, with blatant disregard for human rights and for sinister political reasons, ended up killing innocent people including priests and nuns ministering to the poor in El Salvador, Honduras, Nicaragua, and Guatemala. Nineteen of the twenty-six Salvadoran soldiers who committed the 11/16/89 murders of two women and six Jesuit priests were graduates of the School of the Americas. In 1997, Holstein spent two months in the US federal prison at Lompoc, California, for crossing a line at the Ft. Benning gate in 1995, a second offense for civil disobedience.

Robert Holstein was a major player in the California Democratic Party, a fundraiser for Democrats who wanted to make a difference in the lives of the underserved. He was instrumental in the passage of a 2002 global warming initiative in the California legislature, and of a bill designed to provide health care and education benefits to the poor. On January 9, 2003, State Senator John Burton adjourned the legislature in Holstein's memory. Robert Kaiser, our mutual friend, remembered Bob: "He was a rollicking good, and often profane, storyteller who loved duck hunting and steelhead fishing. He had a cabin near Ft. Jones in the High Sierras that he readily offered to his friends, including Oakland Mayor Jerry Brown, the late House Speaker Tip O'Neill and San Francisco Mayor Willie Brown."

****

Although the world is full of suffering, it is also full of the overcoming of it.
—Helen Keller

Bob Holstein once told me that laughter is a spiritual (that is, fully human) gift of God, a sign of not holding too tightly to grudges, experiencing that it's easier to forgive if you give up unnecessary seriousness, having a wide perspective. Bob's belly-laugh humor didn't demean others but rather, for me, resulted in positive physical and emotional changes in the body, relaxing me to be more engaged. Once he told me he lost his temper and got into a fist fight, on an elevator. Soon after, Bob sought his "enemy" who was totally disarmed when Bob said that he was sorry and somehow, they laughed about it.

The following is the story of Bob's talks with me over the years during which he shared his evolving "spirituality of adoption." Bob strongly advocated for the healing of primal wounds. "Yes, this is so needed," he said. "I support my children's healing—and I advocate for poor traumatized communities. I am focused on the needs of my children and hope to help them undermine the stigma of being an adoptee." Yet, Bob philosophized that our inter-beingness is, perhaps, prior to—and even more fundamental than—blood. Understanding our interconnectedness paradoxically comes back to us as pride in our ancestry, a sense of unique, personal journey. We love and want the best for ourselves, but do not stop with ourselves and extend good will to our neighbors. I admired such a lofty attitude from the observant, rebellious, yet not having all the answers, open to others, humorous brother Jesuit, attorney-at-law Robert Holstein.

Bob was a deeply spiritual and loving person, but he was also a man of his time and culture. He acknowledged that adoption is a trauma, and that an adoptive parent needs to be aware of the trauma and try to feel it, but he thought that the trauma could be transcended through a deep spirituality, through the compassionate affirmation of our common humanity. This may be valid at some ultimate level, but it shouldn't be interpreted in a way that would devalue the adoptee's profound experience of loss. It is important to affirm the priority of the adoptee's painful feelings, which may eventually—through long, hard work—be healed to some extent, but are never erased. Bob's spirituality of adoption is presented here with that caveat.

Bob and I had some "timeless" conversations, meaning they circle back to me to this day, as real to me now as then. They were heart-to-heart exchanges with feeling, about spirituality, religion, activism, and a topic he would invariably bring up: the experience of his adopted children and his experience of being an adoptive parent. Talking face to face, eyes to eyes, giving mutual attention was a way of connecting with Bob and expressed our willingness to face conflicting feelings we usually hid, a vulnerability, a healing honesty.

He was intensely interested in what I felt as an adopted "Irishman." Bob and his kind, sweet, perspicacious wife, Loretta, adopted five children. We had some engrossing conversations that were a kind of therapy for both of us, as well as a bonding to a friend. Bob remarked, "The commitment to compassion and the other is what I enjoy the most. I meditate most days; my faith is not dependent upon a pope, a bishop or anyone else. I validate the presence of God in many of the spiritualities of the world from Native American to Buddhist—it makes no sense otherwise. I am creating my own spirituality of adoption, an openness to appreciating the natural goodness we all possess, whatever our born circumstance and if necessary, to heal whatever keeps us from doing so."

Bob liked to ask me what I "kept hidden," saying that at times he sensed a loneliness in his children even though surrounded by love. At times there would be angry outbursts from one of his children that seemed a reaction to something hurtful in the past, not a response to what was going on in the present, perhaps of being separated from the biological mother years ago? Bob reflected, "My children when angry were, in a way, protecting themselves from rejection." He said yes, there were repercussions for a child separated from her biological mother and father and that we were facing, as friends, emotional roadblocks around adoption together, gaining insight into the power of love to heal the primal wound. "I accept and listen to my children's feelings but know I can only support their individual journeys to overcome the pain from adoption they might experience."

Bob enjoyed hearing about adoptees' social justice projects and approved of the ending of violations of the adoptee's human rights as occurred for those of us born in the '40s and '50s especially. He liked that I wrote the US Attorney General protesting that adopted persons are entitled, as a basic right, to their original birth certificates. A need for me as an adoptee has been to have some feeling for my own genes/heritage/biological parents. The adoptee desires such knowledge, which at the time I could not share with Bob, who always related how he and Loretta loved their adopted children and could appreciate their children's love for them as father and mother as well.

Bob wanted my opinion on issues such as does the adopted child have the right to demand/expect a relationship with the birth mother/birth siblings? (No, if unwanted, I answered.) I do not feel any need or desire to impose on the lives of biological siblings. I have no expectations, nor would I ever close my heart to them. Adoptees have the right to know their nationality, their blood, some circumstances relating to earliest years/relationships, why separation from the mother had to occur and the chance to realize in most cases, the separation does *not imply a lack of love.* Thanking me for being a good listener, Bob related that he could understand his children better after conversing with me about the possible effects of adoption.

Holstein made some good jokes with me about the Irish Catholicism we knew so well. He had great humor about the "sex-negative" "guilt-ridden" messages we were given in our youth. Laughter can be so cathartic. He said he came to observe clearly that women were treated shabbily in the Catholic Church, but that one day there would be acknowledged women priests. We are still waiting. He indignantly related stories of nuns in Ireland in the 1950s, who mistreated children born out of wedlock, in some instances selling them in America to the highest bidder. With disgust, Bob told me how some orphans were forced to work in laundries in Ireland such as in the High Park Laundry from 1954 to 1964 which gained financial profit for the nuns.

Bob expressed that he considered adoption—though certainly not without the need of healing for most adoptees—closer to the reality we are stamped with, encompassing not only the vital ties of blood but those of our very human beingness. Wisely and emotionally, he clarified that we must acknowledge and transform trauma, not spiritually bypass it, not cover it up. Spiritual bypassing is the "tendency to use spiritual ideas and practices to sidestep or avoid facing unresolved emotional issues, psychological wounds, and unfinished developmental tasks." (John Welwood)

We adoptees yearn to be at peace with, and celebrate if possible, our biological roots as well as our relationship to our adoptive parents. Bob suggested that one way to go past trauma, rather than to circumvent it, is through a spirituality rooted in compassionately embracing our inherently shared humanity. He wanted to support his children and me to address, feel, and heal trauma (the necessary psychological process not separate from the spiritual) yet to transcend it by the deep feeling of belonging with and to all people. He emotionally shared his insightful contemplation of inter-being and always already inner goodness (the reality we are each stamped with). Each must find his or her unique way to access a feeling of genuine love of self and interconnectedness.

Such a view broadens—and surely is inclusive of blood ties and adoptive parents—our concept of mother, father, sister, brother. "If one can heal and go past the very real trauma (Why me? How could a mother abandon me? Who am I? What is my racial makeup?) of adoption, which I can only observe—not live—in the intimate moments of my children's musings, their nighttime stories, or telling me their daydreams, one is the beneficiary of short-circuiting the inevitable severing of the umbilicus and finds that one's relatedness is *to the universe and all of humanity.*" Bob spoke of the most basic bond to be to the community of mankind enriched yet unconfined by ties of blood. He felt Jesus was always alluding to this unconditional love and openness for all. Who is my brother? Who is my sister, my mother, my father? He would tell his children that in one sense they were freer than he was, since they could come to realize that "their ties could only be of love, that they need not be cajoled or limited by clan or blood. You always have the opportunity to choose."

A few times we were happily inebriated, secrets exposed more easily, coming unexpectedly like cool summer winds. We shared laughter, stories, our children, talking unabashedly about the struggles of adoption and the healing power of respect, encouragement, patience, and kindness. Bob toasted: "You are my favorite Callahan (Dirty Harry Callahan, portrayed by Clint Eastwood, is second) but even more than Callahan you will also come to know your very genes—because you want and need-deserve that—and I love you like a brother. Cheers to finding you united happily with your blood family as well as with your adopted Irish one (Roman Catholic and all)!"

****

Bob sent me books on Buddhism by Thich Nhat Hanh, who was nominated by Martin Luther King Jr. in 1967 for the Nobel Peace Prize. Thich Nhat Hanh, born in 1926, unfortunately suffered a severe stroke in 2014 and is gravely ill. He influenced Dr. King's decision to vehemently oppose the Vietnam War. They first met in Chicago in 1966 discussing "peace, freedom, and community." The monk and the civil rights leader together condemned the war at a press conference. In June 1965, TNH had written to Dr. King asking for his support to end the Vietnam War. Regarding the Vietnamese monks who set themselves on fire in protest, Thich (Thay) wrote: "Sometimes we have to burn ourselves in order to be heard. It is out of compassion that you do that. It is an act of love and not of despair." I benefitted from *Peace Is Every Step*, about walking meditation, "kissing the Earth with your feet." Paying attention, do what you are doing. Bob sent me the following quote from *Going Home: Jesus and Buddha as Brothers* (1999), which features Buddha and Jesus in an imagined dialogue about their prayer and rituals. "Peace is present right here and now in ourselves and in everything we do and see. We don't have to travel far to enjoy the blue sky. We can smile, breathe, walk, and eat our meals in a way that allows us to be in touch with the abundance of happiness that is available. We need only to be awake, alive in the present moment."

****

I was invited to volunteer with a Christian church that travels twice a year to San Tecla, Mexico, home to a sister church which serves Indigenous Oaxacans. Indigenous workers travel north for a better salary of about $8.00 a day, which is twice what they can earn in Oaxaca, if work is even available. One member of the church was my coworker, Margot, at Mission Lodge Sanitarium in San Gabriel, California. Over the years, I helped Margot with some fundraising, which Bob supported. He said, "Someday we will go together." It wasn't until Christmas vacation 2003 that, thinking of Bob as my spiritual companion, I accompanied church members to enjoy good company with sisters and brothers south of the border. We arrived at the large ranch early in the chilly morning to organize presents for children, clothes and food baskets for families. We had driven two and a half hours from the seaport of Ensenada, located on Bahía de Todos

Santos, sixty miles south of Tijuana. There was a rousing Christian service, with around 120 children sitting in front of the church's stage, which featured musicians, women preachers and singers, melodies with electric guitars and percussion beats. We weave and sway, swooning with Jesus.

Dios Es Amor is painted in large white letters on an impressive brown cross. The sun is shining its bright yellow into the rocking church. Children go to some small arts and crafts classes, while the adults receive bags of beans, rice, sugar, clothes, soap, shampoo. It's very cold outside; some of the shivering children still don't have shoes, so the church members make sure they are given sneakers and a warm puffy jacket. As with our own children, it's a joy seeing a youngster receiving a gift, a spontaneous beaming response. I'm thinking fondly of my grandchildren, Penelope and Morgan, who jubilantly gather each Christmas with friends, cousins, and family to give and receive gifts, an endearing emotionally bonding circle of love.

Generous volunteers realize they are receiving one of those small, fleeting satisfactions that feed our souls. Seven of us take a quick dirt-road truck ride to view the ocean, speeding past the tomato plants, which the Oaxacan Indians are covering with plastic to protect from the bitter cold sea winds. We stay on the hilly shore for thirty minutes, slipping on wet rocks, mostly gray, some ivory-colored blotched with rust, white and brown corrugated clam shells, delicate detached crab legs; waves spray salty water on me. I take a handful of ocean water to splash on my face to remember Bob for his aliveness and life-changing kindness to me.

In the next four chapters, I will tell what has been revealed to me about Lionel Durand and provide some samples of the articles he wrote as an ace reporter.

9

Embracing Lionel Durand

Lionel Durand's interests were legion; so were his talents. Counting Picasso among his intimate friends, he was himself a painter of quality, a nimble guitarist, and fluent in six languages. He could cover a Khrushchev press conference one day and bullfighting in Spain the next. But the big story for Durand was always politics. One of the first to predict de Gaulle's return to power, Durand was still covering a part of the de Gaulle story when he went to Africa to cover the Algerian war. He visited the Casbah to interview Moslem leaders during one of the riots and was caught in a crossfire as police tried to quell the disturbance. Though a tear-gas bomb exploded at his feet he went, coughing and sputtering, half-walking, half-running, to file his story from a cable office miles away. He returned to the Paris bureau exhausted, the tear gas having added to the strain of the previous months.

He knew Paris as well as he knew the keyboard of his battered typewriter; he brought it alive in his cables, and there was never an American visitor who wanted a glass of wine, or a wise briefing on French politics, or a gay laugh in a bistro, who did not get it freely from him. This was Lionel Durand.
—Haiti Sun, January 29, 1961

This story—though I am ever curious to keep learning—marks the end of a search to know Lionel Durand, a gift full of revelatory and healing Light.

Born in Port-au-Prince on December 22, 1920, baby Lionel Durand emerged in a Haiti controlled by the USA. In 1915, Haitian president Jean Vilbrun Guillaume Sam was assassinated, throwing the country into chaos. Woodrow Wilson sent Marines to establish political and economic order. $500,000 was transferred from Haiti's national bank to New York, and pro-American Philippe Sudré Dartiguenave was made president. Disgracefully, Dartiguenave did not represent the best interests of the Haitian people. A new constitution was written in 1917 allowing foreign land ownership; it was a time of forced labor, censoring of the press, and racial segregation. The US occupation would last until 1934.

Lionel's father, Louis Durand (born 1863), was a prewar Haitian ambassador to France. He had three children in Haiti, one of whom died in a war. Later in life he moved to France. Louis went back to Haiti from France and remarried with a Haitian woman (Madeleine de Pradines, born 1892). Louis and Madeleine had three children: Lionel, Réne, and Andrée. In the 1942 ship's manifest, Louis is listed as having lived in NYC from 1911–1917; his second wife was recorded as being in New York from 1915–1917, so they probably married in 1915. My patriotic grandfather Louis even purchased and outfitted a yacht/warship in New England, USA, and sent it to the Haitian Capital, Port-au-Prince, to support the government from being overthrown. The US Press had a field day with this armed yacht!

In 1910, Louis served in France as the General Consul. Louis had quite a career—and so did his son Lionel Durand, who prepared himself well, studied at the Sorbonne, Heidelberg, and Oxford, and spoke French, English, German, Russian, Spanish (as, enjoyably, do I), and Italian. Far away, but attuned to Haiti, Lionel would live his youth mostly in France.

In *Newsweek's* obituary, an original January 24, 1961 copy in my hand, cover photo of newly inaugurated John F. Kennedy in a classy black top hat, Lionel was hailed as a first-class newsman and a *good* man. "To all the men and women of *Newsweek*, and to the mountain climbers and statesmen, the actors, artists, writers, teachers, singers, diplomats, and elevator operators who counted themselves his friends, Durand was more than a first-class reporter. He was kindness, resourcefulness, generosity, humor, and courage—and those are the qualities for which he will be missed."

The *New York Times* also praised Lionel in its obituary, "Lionel Durand, a Newsman Dies," *New York Times*, January 15, 1961, recounting that Lionel Durand was a former member of the French Resistance who was "twice arrested by the Gestapo and twice escaped." Lionel faced the added difficulties for Blacks fighting in the French Resistance. Former resistance fighter, Philippe de Vomécourt wrote in 1961: "For coloured men in France, a 'safe house' or false identity papers were an impossibility. To be a coloured man in a district occupied by the Germans was to know that death was near. The Germans had a pathological fear and hatred of coloured men." Yet Lionel resisted and bravely fought!

✳✳✳✳✳✳✳

In May and June of 1940 when the German army was fighting in France, they encountered Black African soldiers who had been recruited by the French army. For the most part, German troops treated White POWs according to the mandates of the Geneva Convention (1929). Being Black however—*they are just savages*—was dangerous, as Blacks were considered subhuman. "Germans dealt with the Black Africans in a way that anticipated the horrors of the racialized warfare associated with the later German campaigns in the Balkans and the Soviet Union. In close combat, German units fought against Black soldiers of the French army with a ruthlessness that suggested that no prisoners would be taken. On many occasions, Black prisoners of war were shot—sometimes up to several hundred at a time. When Germans did not kill Black prisoners outright, they often separated them from the White French captives and subjected them to harsh treatment." (*The Journal of Modern History*, "German Massacre of Black Soldiers from the French Army," R. Scheck, 2005)

Black women, such as Jane Vialle (1906-1953) and Eugénie Eboué (1891-1972), like Lionel Durand, made outstanding contributions to the fight against the Nazis. Jane Vialle, daughter of a French father and African mother, was born in Ouesco, Republic of the Congo. Her father returned to France when Jane was seven years old. Like Lionel, she became a journalist. At the start of the war, she moved from Paris to Marseille and became an agent (information services) with one of the three principal Resistance movements in the South of France. Just as Lionel did, she escaped from a Nazi prison. "In January 1943 she was charged with treason, tried, and convicted. She was incarcerated for four months in the Brens women's concentration camp and then transferred to the Beaumettes women's prison in Marseille until December 1943. Some sources, including the French government itself, indicate that Vialle escaped from prison." (*Black Perspectives*, "From Concentration Camps to the Senate: Black Women in the French Resistance," Annette Joseph-Gabriel, March 13, 2017)

Eugénie Eboué was born in French Guyana and married Felix Eboué in 1922. She received the Medal of Resistance. "At the start of World War II, she joined the Women's Army Auxiliary Corps and was stationed as a nurse at the Brazzaville military hospital until 1944. Her contributions to the war effort and subsequent political activism earned her at least twenty-six medals of recognition." ("From Concentration Camps to the Senate: Black Women in the French Resistance") Both Eugénie and Jane were voted to serve in the French Senate where they addressed the problem of colonialism, advocating for legislation that would protect the rights of women in France's colonies. Vialle "pursued legislation that would change France's paternity laws in order to increase state protections for otherwise unrecognized mixed-race children and by extension their African mothers. . . . Both women were also active in a Black internationalist project and made connections between liberation struggles in Africa, the Antilles, and the United States. . . . During her time in the United States, Vialle was the NAACP's guest of honor and was also featured in what was known then as a Negro History Week kit. She was the only woman in a lineup of Black internationalist figures, including Carter G. Woodson, W. E. B. DuBois, emperor Haile Selassie, and Felix Eboué."

I imagine Lionel Durand met and enjoyed performances by the "Creole Goddess" "Black Venus" of France, celebrated Jazz Age entertainer, dancer, singer, actress, spy for the Resistance, Josephine Baker (1906–1975). At Paris cafes, virtuoso word-crafter Ernest Hemingway (1899–1961) enjoyed libations and conversations with the vivaciously effusive Josephine, infusing Hemingway with her juicy personality, calling her "the most sensational woman anybody ever saw. Or ever will."

Eavesdrop for yourself as you read this passage from the book, *Hemingway in Love: His Own Story* by A. E. Hotchner, who recorded Ernest's fascinating stories about his shaky love life. When interviewed, Hemingway was staying in the psychiatric ward at St. Mary's Hospital, and a few weeks after dictating this memoir, Ernest died from a self-inflicted Scott double-barreled 12-gauge gunshot wound to the head.

"I couldn't take my eyes off a beautiful woman on the dance floor—tall, coffee skin, ebony eyes, long seductive legs: Very hot night, but she was wearing a black fur coat. The woman and I introduced ourselves. Her name was Josephine Baker, an American. Said she was about to open at the Folies Bergère, that she had just come from rehearsal. I asked why the fur on a warm night in June. She slid open her coat for a moment to show she was naked. 'I just threw something on,' she said, 'we don't wear much at the Folies. Why don't you come? I'm headlining as the ebony goddess.' I spent that night with Josephine, sitting at her kitchen table, drinking champagne sent by an admirer. I carried on nonstop about my trouble. . . . Josephine listened, intense, sympathetic. She was a hell of a listener. She said she too had suffered from double love. The rest of that night, into dawn, we talked about our souls."

No wonder Lionel's friend, Picasso, was so attracted to draw paintings of the alluring Josephine. On the Internet, well worth enjoying, are many paintings and drawings depicting the indomitable Josephine Baker.

Watching sensual, rhythmical, dazzling, deep-voiced Josephine perform (sometimes in a banana skirt!) on YouTube is a treat and a tribute to her lasting impact on the world. But her life as a child was difficult, insecure, cold, unanchored, and sad. Josephine grew up in St. Louis,

Missouri; she never knew the identity of her biological father. At age 13, Josephine was living on the street in a cardboard shell, dancing on street corners for meager coins. Yet by 1925, she was sailing to Paris (19 years old and raring to go); Josephine was on her way to conquering merry Paris and wide audiences throughout Europe, embarking on a 50-year career of performing. She became a star of the *Folies Bergère* and *La Revue Nègre*. There was no stopping her; in 1930, in Paris, she recorded her signature song *J'ai Deux Amours*. Josephine would have her glorious time in the sun but the lavish party in less than a decade would come to a startling halt.

Tragically, in 1939, came Hitler's evil unleashing of Nazi soldiers and vicious weapons upon Poland (September 1, 1939–October 6, 1939). The Soviet Union would invade on September 17; the two bully countries (along with Lithuania and the Slovak client-state), after their short brutal bloody battle, divided the spoils, annexing a broken, devastated and enslaved Poland. A Polish survivor, Victor Bik, wrote a memoir, relating what it was like to be attacked that infamous day, a bitter happening seared forever into his psyche.

"The *Schleswig-Holstein* (German warship) had been docked at the Polish harbor feigning a friendship visit, but at 4:45 a.m. that day the battleship opened fire on Poland's Fort Westerplatte barracks, which bunked more than one hundred sleeping men.... The garrison of 182 Polish soldiers returned fire on the 3,000 Germans.... What lay in store for the teenage Bik at the end of the 27-day war in Poland was an experience in a wartime slave operation. 'The sound of bombs and explosions broke into my town and destroyed it. The horrors of war followed ... people were beaten, tortured, executed by firing squads, or hung in the streets. For a teenage boy, these things were unthinkable.'

Shortly after the United States entered the war, Bik was con-
scripted by the Nazi SS and taken to work in forced labor.
Bik escaped from forced-labor camps twice and in 1944 was
arrested as a political prisoner for doing so. 'With wire
around my wrists, I was thrown into a boxcar and transported to Gross-Rosen concentration camp.' Liberated from
Bergen-Belsen concentration camp, Bik says he tells his
story with the hope that people will listen and do everything
in their power to prevent such things from happening
again." (*Herald-Tribune*, "70 Years after Invasion, a Polish
Survivor Remembers," Catherine A. Hamilton, September
1, 2009)

As a response to Hitler's invasion of Poland, in 1939 the
charming Josephine was recruited by French military intelligence. Josephine was to get vital information, such as the
location of German troops, from the loosened lips of party-
ing Japanese and Italian military leaders, enchanted by Josephine at their embassies. In 1940, Germany entered Paris
and Josephine fled to southern France, where she opened
her house to members of the Free Forces, providing them
visas. As an entertainer, she could travel to neutral countries
such as those in South America or Portugal. She carried documents to be sent to England. Notes were written in invisible ink on her sheet music. (*Jazz Cleopatra: Josephine Baker
in Her Time*, Phyllis Rose, 1989)

Josephine accompanied Dr. Martin Luther King Jr. on
his 1963 March on Washington, the only official woman
speaker. In her speech, she acknowledged Rosa Parks and
thundered to the captivated audience: "I have walked into
the palaces of kings and queens and into the houses of pres-
idents. But I could not walk into a hotel in America and get
a cup of coffee, and that made me mad, and when I get mad,
you know that I open my big mouth. And then look out,

'cause when Josephine opens her mouth, they hear it all over the world."

And White women—in solidarity with their Black sisters—did their grand part as well. In the riveting book written by Sonia Purnell about Virginia Hall (1906-1982), *A Woman of Importance: The Untold Story of the American Spy Who Helped Win World War II*, Purnell states that the relatively few Blacks in France were specifically targeted by the Nazis. The adventurous Baltimore socialite Virginia, who accidentally shot herself in the foot when she was 27, losing her left leg from the knee down to gangrene (no antibiotics at the time), exemplified how French Resistance fighters, men and women, contributed to overcoming Hitler's pernicious plan of world domination. Even with a prosthetic leg, which Virginia whimsically named Cuthbert, she was not held back, but went to France in August 1941 to work—with a license to kill—first for the UK's SOE (Special Operations Executive) and later the OSS (Office of Strategic Services). She became the Gestapo's (Nazi police) most wanted agent in France as she set up spy networks (spoke five languages), arranged transportation of secret documents, and provided resources, such as arms and money for agents, ambushes, explosives, jail escapes, protection for downed Allied airmen, reconnaissance, and sabotage.

The Durands were residing in the strategic port town of Le Havre on the eastern side of the Seine Bay, captured by the Nazis in May 1940. The Le Havre Resistance was centered around branches such as the group of Le Havre High School and the *Vagabond Bien-Aimé (Beloved Vagabond)*, which were involved with British Intelligence and with acts of sabotage up until the Normandy Invasion on June 6, 1944. The besieged people of Le Havre had to suffer food and supplies shortages, bombings, censorship, arrests, and political anti-Semitism. Resistance soldiers—small cells of armed women and men—fought against the Nazis and the collaborative Vichy Regime in guerilla warfare, by sharing intelligence with the Allies, writing underground newspapers, which Lionel most certainly must have written for (the pen being mighty beside the sword), providing escape routes for Allied soldiers caught behind enemy lines, and sabotaging electrical power grids and telecommunication networks.

On August 23, 1941, Haiti banned Nazi consuls, announcing the withdrawal of all privileges of German consuls "for internal and international reasons." Haiti closed its consulates in Germany and German-occupied countries such as France, where Louis Durand was Haitian Ambassador. Haiti-Nazi relations completely ended when, on August 25, Germany's government announced that all Haitian consulates in Germany would be closed by September 15. Nazi consuls in Haiti were to be withdrawn also by September 15.

It was urgent that Lionel, who had been arrested twice, and his family leave Nazi-occupied France. Eventually arriving in New York City on June 30, 1942, Lionel was appointed French section director of Voice of America. With the intent to fight Nazi propaganda, Voice of America began February 1, 1942 with a broadcast from a small studio in NYC to Germany. "The news may be good or bad; we shall tell you the truth." Lionel continued to resist the evil intents of Adolf Hitler.

****

In recognition of, and to honor my father's war service — how I would like to know how he escaped twice from the Gestapo!—in the French Resistance under the Nazi Occupation, John Suggs obtained for me an authentic Resistance medal. Hanging on my wall, I view the medal with reverence and pride.

The Resistance medal is the actual decoration bestowed by the French Committee of National Liberation based in the United Kingdom during World War II. It was established by a decree of General Charles de Gaulle on February 9, 1943 *to recognize the remarkable acts of faith and courage that, in France, in the empire and abroad, have contributed to the resistance of the French people against the enemy and against its accomplices since June 18, 1940.* The Resistance medal is a 37 mm in diameter circular medal struck from bronze. Its slightly concave obverse displays at center its principal design, a vertical Cross of Lorraine with the relief semicircular inscription of the date of General de Gaulle's appeal of June 18, 1940, "XVIII.VI.MCMXL" (18.06.1940) bisected by the lower part of the cross. The reverse bears the relief image of an unfurling ribbon with the relief inscription in Latin "*PATRIA NON IMMEMOR,*" The nation does not forget. The suspension is cast as an integral part of the medal. The Resistance medal hangs from a 36 mm wide black silk moiré (wavy texture) ribbon with six vertical red stripes of varying widths, 3 mm wide edge stripes, two 1 mm wide central stripes 2 mm apart, and two 1 mm wide stripes 6 mm from the central stripes.

Now treasured by me on behalf of my father, and which I will pass on to my stepson David, the Resistance medal was awarded to approximately 38,288 living persons and 24,463 posthumously.

****

The FBI investigated the recently NYC-arrived Durands. In a letter from J. Edgar Hoover, it was ascertained that Louis

Durand, the Haitian Consul in La Havre, France, returned to his home on July 16, 1941 and encountered four German soldiers who demanded his passports and those of his family. The soldiers refused to give him a receipt for the passports and confiscated the following: diplomatic passports and passports of Durand's family; exequatur and act of nomination by Haitian Government; marriage certificate of Durand's son, Lionel; official and private letters; all consular seals; blank passports; and notes belonging to Lionel and a photograph.

In 1942 when Lionel, his wife Yolande, and his sister Andrée arrived in NYC with their father and mother, the ship's manifest says that their closest relative was Lionel's older brother Réne, who was still living in France. Lionel's first marriage on June 15, 1941 to Yolande Françoise Bemova (1920–2005) was arranged, a *mariage blanc*, to enable his bride to escape, for unknown reasons, from Vichy France and get to the US; records show they did not live together after they arrived in NYC. In fact, she was living on Park Avenue; clearly, she had resources. The marriage was annulled on August 17, 1945 by the Supreme Court of New York. Yolande needed the State Department to confirm the annulment so that she could access her father's estate in France. She had renounced her French citizenship for Haitian citizenship as a requirement of her marriage to Lionel.

According to their records, Lionel and Yolande were married a full year before they got out of France. Did they backdate the time of their marriage or were they really trying for a full year to escape the Nazis while faking their marriage? That long? And wouldn't it be risky in occupied France for Yolande to be married to a Black man? Even if he had diplomatic cover as the Ambassador's "secretary"? Who would think it was safer for Yolande to be seen as a White woman marrying a Black man? And since Lionel had been captured and escaped the Gestapo twice, why would he be a solid bet for her to fake a marriage with? How many Black men were active and known in the French Resistance? He could have been readily and easily identified and picked up just by his skin color alone. So many questions! Too few answers.

In the Congressional Record, the US State Department submitted a list of foreign journalists in 1949 who had press credentials at the US State Department. Lionel is listed as a reporter for the *Paris-Presse*, a French afternoon daily, and so had access to the most desired stories.

Lionel returned to a long-liberated France in 1956, where he became the foreign editor of *Paris-Presse*, and eventually joined *Newsweek*. Lionel was regarded as a "correspondent who understood both the people he was reporting on and the people—the American people—he was reporting to." Lionel wrote articles for American publications on Parisian art, music (knew opera directors), and culture. I am holding the March 1960 *Theater Arts* magazine in which Lionel's article, "Opera, Paris" appears. He writes about the comeback of the Paris Opera, which had suffered "a long string of mediocre performances." It seems that, at the time, the storied Opera House had a bad reputation. "In February 1958, Paris went without opera performances for several weeks at the height of the season. Stagehands, who wanted a raise, had called for a strike; one thing leading to another in that highly explosive milieu, three hundred of the Opera's staff of 1100 had been fired. But *Paris-Journal* noted with sadness, no one seemed to care."

As *Newsweek*'s Paris bureau chief, Lionel was assigned a variety of interesting stories that took him around the world:

de Gaulle in France, Khrushchev and school children in Russia, Ingemar "Hammer of Thor" Johansson (KO'd Floyd Patterson in 1959, becoming heavyweight boxing champion) in Geneva.

Ben Bradlee (1921–2014), close friends with the Kennedy family, was *Newsweek*'s post-war Paris bureau chief; he hired Lionel to work with him. Bradlee wrote *Conversations with Kennedy* and *A Good Life: Newspapering and other Adventures,* in which he expresses his appreciation for Lionel, who was invited to Bradlee's wedding party.

"To be blunt about it, I didn't know anything about blacks or the black experience, and I was about to become involved in the leadership of the number one newspaper in a city (Washington, DC) that was 70 percent black and a readership that was 25 percent black. I had only one black friend as a grown-up, my *Newsweek* colleague, Lionel Durand, in Paris. . . . Members of the party included . . . Lionel and Toto (Irène) Durand. . . . Lionel Durand was one of the most remarkable men I ever met. He was my 'assistant,' which does him no justice at all, since he was twice as smart as I was about most things, certainly about all things French. He used the French familiar to Picasso. . . . He knew the leaders of the burgeoning French film industry, the literary shots big and small . . . incredibly well connected, especially to the cultural scene, where I struggled. He was a fabulous asset to me and to *Newsweek*. We traveled to the *Place des Vosges,* trailing tin cans from our car, courtesy of Durand who knew full well that the French had no such custom. And we drank bottle after bottle of champagne, toasting the miracle we had pulled off and the start of our great adventure."

10

What's the Scoop?

No tears in the writer, no tears in the reader. No surprise in the writer, no surprise in the reader.
—Robert Frost

Words can be like X-rays if you use them properly—they'll go through anything. You read and you're pierced.
—Aldous Huxley

The purpose of a writer is to keep civilization from destroying itself.
—Albert Camus

On November 10, 1948, *The Circleville Herald* (Circleville, Pickaway, Ohio), published "Paris Newspaper Insists Truman, Stalin Talk Set." It said that rumors persisted that President Truman would meet with Premier Stalin if the Berlin crisis was not settled by year's end. The Paris newspaper account from Washington cited White House denials but there were wide rumors that the President had decided on such a meeting if the United Nations failed to achieve a settlement on the blockade issue. "Another article by Lionel Durand, *Paris-Presse* foreign editor, says information from an American source indicates the President plans to seek a new basis of American policy toward Russia. Durand adds that certain White House advisors frankly are urging a different attitude toward Moscow which could bring a new conciliation effort at the highest levels of the two governments."

At the end of World War II, fallen Germany was divided into sections controlled by the USA, Britain, France, and the Soviet Union at the Yalta Conference from February 4 to February 11, 1945, and confirmed at Potsdam, July 17 to August 2, 1945. Angry that West Berlin established the Deutsche Mark as its currency, the Soviet Union set a blockade from June 24, 1948 to May 12, 1949, denying the Allies access to Berlin by road, railway, and canal. The Allies of the US, Britain, France, Australia, Canada, South Africa, and New Zealand carried out two hundred thousand Berlin airlift sorties to get supplies, food, and fuel to the people.

Truman and Stalin never talked. Thrown into full throttle, the Cold War was underway. West Germany triumphantly would join NATO in 1955.

****

Lionel reported on French rule in Vietnam in the early 1950s. John Suggs mused: "He would have really *made his mark* covering the US involvement in Vietnam if he had lived beyond 1961. Just think. He would have been in his 40s during the 1960s, and would have really come into his own professionally. One of the biggest stories of the decade was Vietnam, and Lionel was a clear expert on it from his reporting in the 1950s for France. He even quotes a French leader who wanted to negotiate directly with Ho Chi Minh!"

When Lionel wrote his March 16, 1954 report, "New French Plan for Indochina," the Vietminh had already been fighting French Union Forces for eight years. "The near unanimous desire in France is to end the long-drawn $4,000,000,000 war."

"The Battle for France," an article written by Lionel for *The New Republic* (June 1951), gives an incisive, smart analysis of France's June 17, 1951 legislative election. A skillful newsman, Lionel clearly had his finger on the pulse of French post-war politics. Especially de Gaulle. He was 31 years old and was obviously spending a big part of his life in France at this tumultuous time, though still based in NYC. "In just a few days, on June 17, the French people will go to the polls to elect a new Assembly to replace the one which, since November 1946, has made it hard for any coalition government to rule." One third of the legislative body was controlled by the Communist Party. To complicate matters, there were two thousand candidates and 14 national parties each of which would be allotted 10 minutes on live public radio for electoral propaganda. "Sharp differences between the other parties have forced eight successive cabinets out of existence in less than five years."

The campaign would be short and bitter, with billboards and political posters put up, torn down, put up again. Yet factions in the Assembly who fought each other over such issues as social security and the Vietnam War "are now eager to stand together for another five-year ride." The times called for governmental stability. The Socialists and Christian Democrats stressed domestic issues such as economic growth by fortifying the value of the franc abroad and by building upon the "country's comeback since the war and the occupation." The Communists parroted Soviet slogans for "peace" and against "German rearmament, the war in Indo-China, and the American invasion." Some pundits claimed that de Gaulle, the great wartime leader, had "lost touch with the people." But "his opponents do not underestimate his potential appeal as an honest man with complete integrity, little interest in money, and an uncompromising record as a staunch fighter for French prestige abroad. Can General de Gaulle succeed in convincing the large group of people who still see in him a potential dictator?"

Lionel wrote that the election might be "de Gaulle's last chance to play an important part in France's political life." De Gaulle founded the Rally of the French People (RPF) party in 1947. In the election, the RPF successfully gained some power to combat the Communist party by winning 120 seats in the National Assembly. By 1953, however, de Gaulle severed ties with the RPF, which disbanded in 1955. From 1955 to 1956, de Gaulle retired from public appearances to write his memoirs. Lionel correctly predicted that *le grand Charles* would return to power, and he did indeed become president of France on January 8, 1959.

****

In 1957, Durand was among the first reporters from the West to talk to Nikita Sergeyevich Khrushchev (1894–1971), who was the First Secretary of the Communist Party from 1953 to 1964. An impressed John Suggs commented, "It was the time of Sputnik; that was a real scoop! Lionel was a helluva reporter!"

Lionel was covering the four-day and four-night celebration of Bolshevism's fortieth anniversary. Long-winded Nikita got things rolling with a three-hour speech to 17,000 Communists from 61 nations. He bragged that Communism had become a "mighty world system."

"His sputniks launched, and his rule secure, at least momentarily, Nikita S. Khrushchev was wheeling and dealing for strength, rattling rockets, and talking peace on Soviet terms."

NSK liked also to have a blast. "Khrushchev was the life of the party. He waltzed with a blonde and sang the *Marsellaise* at a Kremlin party of 3,000."

Lionel visited a Russian school where Russian stories and discipline were inculcated. In an English class, a 14-year-old girl asked Lionel in good English: "I study English at school. Do American girls of my age study Russian?" The electromagnetic shop was busy with boys and girls "turning out industrial tools with modern machinery." Did the teacher feel, Lionel inquired, that it was "more important to make children happy or to make them useful?" The teacher replied with deep conviction, "How can they be happy if they are not useful?"

****

Lionel, a painter himself, was a close friend of Pablo Picasso. Such a fascinating relationship must have fortified his creative juices to write important magazine and newspaper stories, not to mention an exhilarating ramping up of his social life. When *Newsweek* did a picture story on Picasso's London exhibition, Pablo supplied his own captions for Lionel's photographs. "I did this," explained Picasso, "out of friendship for Lionel."

The prodigious Picasso (1881–1973), who drew before he could walk, was most definitely an artistic marvel. The 1956 movie (the year Lionel returned to Paris from NYC), *Le mystère Picasso*, "The Mystery of Picasso," directed by

Henri-Georges Clouzot, takes us into Pablo's studio where
we are invited to participate as Picasso creates paintings for
the camera right before our eyes, fresh spontaneous images
filling our senses and piquing our sensibilities. We see Picasso in one scene—smoking a cigarette, in shorts and san-
dals, no shirt—drawing one black curve after another: "For
the first time, the daily and private drama of the blind genius
will be experienced publicly . . . In the darkness of the canvas, the light slowly appears." Who can say what Muse was
"guiding the creator through his perilous adventures?" Picasso reflected on the mysterious, mostly unconscious
source of creativity in a closeup shot of his entranced eyes:
"One would die to know what was on Rimbaud's mind when
writing a poem." Wanting to keep the paintings limited only
through viewing the film, most of the paintings were destroyed.

In the summer of 1987, I visited Museo Reina Sofia in
Madrid, Spain to see Picasso's 1937 heart wrenching, anti-
war oil painting, 11 feet tall and 25.6 ft. wide masterpiece,
Guernica. Picasso was recreating before my widened eyes in
bleak blue-black-white the horror inflicted on the city of
Guernica bombed by the Nazis during the Spanish Civil
War, resulting in the destruction of three-quarters of the
Basque town, killing and maiming hundreds of civilians. I
could decipher a skull superimposed over the horse's body,
whose tongue was replaced by three daggers. A bull is
formed from the horse's bent leg. Taking in a screaming
mother holding her dead child, along with agonized dying
adults, children, and animals, I felt the daggers cutting into
my spirit. A Minotaur symbolizes irrational unrestrained
mad destructive power, and the Harlequin represents tran-
scendence of life and death, the life-affirming alternative to
the deaths and mayhem inflicted by the Nazis. Pablo had
been living in Paris for years when the bombing took place.

A German officer who saw a photo of *Guernica* asked: "Did you do that?" Picasso allegedly replied, "No, you did."

Both Pablo and Lionel fought against the Nazis in their unique ways and that may well have been the source of their mutual respect.

****

As a former French Resistance fighter, Lionel "knew most of the major figures of that heroic era, up to and including President de Gaulle." I imagine Lionel interviewing and chatting with de Gaulle about world politics.

On May 19, 1954 Lionel typed the headline "Saar is a Political No-Man's Land." He quotes a realistic General Charles de Gaulle (1890–1970), the self- assured leader who led the Free French Forces against Adolf Hitler in World War II and later became President and architect of France's Fifth Republic (1958–1969), as he crossed the industrial Saar Basin by train.

"What will be done with these people? There is only one thing certain. Nobody is going to turn them into Frenchmen." I reflected how vital one's blood and genetic makeup is for the identity of a person and group of people. Though under the power of the French, the people were proud to be German, nourished by German uniqueness and so not wanting to be economically and politically controlled, not wanting to adopt the French culture.

The Treaty of Versailles had taken Saar (borders France and was a major source of coal for Germany) from Germany, given to the League of Nations and occupied by the United Kingdom and France for fifteen years (1920-1935);

its coalfields were ceded to France who ran the lucrative coal mines and iron and metal processing businesses. Many anti-Hitler Germans fled to Saar after 1933 (population 812,000), the only territory of Germany under foreign occupation. They actively rallied for Saar to remain under French and English control, free from the need to be subservient to the vicious Nazi dictator. In 1935 it would be Hitler who would brag about a German victory: the Saar region voted 90% to return to German control.

In 1945, after World War II, the French, backed by French military forces, once again controlled the coveted German territory. In 1947, the first Saar state parliament ratified a constitution that called for an autonomous Saar in an economic union with France. But meanwhile, by 1954, West Germany was flying high. The 1954 World Cup soccer champs (though later found to have been cheating by doping) were a perfect symbol for the prosperous and culturally dynamic West Germany. Saar wanted to be a part of Germany again, part of the *homeland* living the full life like in West Germany with its freedom of expression, inventiveness, sterling optimism, finally overcoming the ruins to body and soul of the horrid war. Hitler had "scorched the earth," obliterating 20% of all housing. But by 1954, people declared that West Germany was an economic miracle!

In October 1956, the Saar Treaty authorized Saarland to again join Germany, which finalized on January 1, 1957.

****

I contemplated, felt touched by an unusual encounter—let your own colorful imagination come into play—between Lionel and H.D. (Hilda Doolittle, 1884–1961). They were impacted by each other at the end of their lives.

Born in Bethlehem, Pennsylvania, Hilda Doolittle was an accomplished poet, friends with William Butler Yeats (Irish) and Ezra Pound (expatriate American). Like these master poets, Hilda drew inner nourishment from reading-discussing-writing poetry, getting published and becoming well known, confident, adventurous, cultivating psychological and spiritual depth, imbibing the intuitive wisdom of varied cultures and their myths and contemplative practices, Jung-Freud, magic, mystical Christianity and Eastern religion, Greek and Egyptian lore.

Hilda was spreading her wings and gliding away from Victorian proprieties and dogmatic certainties.

"Isis takes many forms, as does Osiris," Hilda wrote. The goddess Isis was the consort of Osiris, god of the underworld. Beautiful in a sheath dress, a solar disc and cow horns on her head, Isis saves Osiris who was murdered, his body torn into fourteen pieces, scattered throughout Egypt. Isis and her sister carefully buried all the pieces except for the phallus, which they preserved to give invigorated life to Osiris. Thus empowered, Osiris remained judge and ruler of the underworld. In what way did Isis (Hilda) and Osiris (Lionel) uplift each other? We can only fantasize.

Thirty-seven years Lionel's senior, Doolittle was a major player in writing twentieth-century avant-garde poetry. *Newsweek's* Lionel Durand went to interview H.D. in April 1960 in Zurich, after Hilda's completing *Bid Me to Live.* Then they met in NYC in May 1960 when she received the gold medal for poetry from the American Academy of Arts and Letters. Doolittle conversed with a charismatic Durand, a "Haitian," comparing him to 1960 gold medalist decathlon superstar, Rafer Johnson (1934–2020). Doolittle pictured Rafer as a heroic good-looking, muscular, shining god of

Olympia. Hilda proclaimed, "Women are seeking, as one woman, fragments of the Eternal Lover." Lionel—handsome, 6'2", dark, radiating wide-eyed bright listening—became a shining fragment. I read some intriguing poems from *Hermetic Definition: Poetry by Hilda Doolittle*, written between 1957 and 1961. Hermetic definition means establishing an openness of mind and heart based upon ancient wisdom. In the following, Hilda offers Lionel a lyrical complaint full of love.

> *Why did you come*
> *to trouble my decline?*
> *I am old (I was old till you came)*
> *the reddest rose unfolds*
> *(which is ridiculous*
> *in this time, this place*
> *unseemly, impossible*
> *even slightly scandalous),*
> *the reddest rose unfolds*

H.D. From *Red Rose and a Beggar* (August 17–August 24, 1960)

****

As his last hurrah, Lionel Durand contributed to three stories in *Newsweek*, January 24, 1961: "The Periscope," p. 9–10; "On NATO," p. 26; "Belgium, The Showdown," p. 40.

Here are a few striking international news headlines in "The Periscope." *From the Pentagon*, President Kennedy looking to end the 27-month US moratorium on nuclear tests in order to "prod the Soviets into getting down to serious business on disarmament and safeguards against surprise attack." *From East Berlin*, reports there was an explosion in Red China's Sinkiang nuclear research center, where China was trying to build its first atomic bomb. Successfully testing its atomic bomb just three years later on October 16, 1964, China joined the Soviet Union, the US, the UK, and France in possessing such an immensely destructive nuclear weapon. And, finally, *From Tunis*, Paris ready to sign an agreement to turn its big navy base at Bizerte over to Tunisia much sooner than originally planned. This in reward for Tunisian President Bourguiba's efforts to "moderate the Algerian rebel demands and his backing to de Gaulle as the best man to end the Algerian war."

In "On NATO," Lionel begins, "One hundred and ten miles behind the Iron Curtain lies a city that the West can neither defend nor give up. This is West Berlin, so often threatened by Communist siege that much of the world is tired of hearing about it. But by the time Caroline Kennedy is rolling Easter eggs on the White House lawn, a new Berlin crisis is virtually certain. What will the West do then?" Lionel lists the players. The British want to negotiate a new status for the city, and John Kennedy said he would agree if the Russians made concessions. Charles de Gaulle wants to maintain Western troops in Berlin even if by force. Germany's Chancellor Konrad Adenauer wants neither to concede anything nor to have a crisis. "Such discord dramatizes a more basic problem facing Mr. Kennedy. At the heart of the problem is NATO." Lionel relates that Secretary-General Paul-Henri Spaak says the alliance must combat Russia's economic offensive in the underdeveloped world. "The objection: NATO aid might smack of 'colonialism'. Supreme Commander in Europe, Gen. Lauris Norstad says NATO should acquire its own nuclear weapons. The objection: It might intensify the arms race."

The North Atlantic Treaty Organization (NATO), signed on April 4, 1949, is an intergovernmental military alliance between 30 North American and European countries agreeing to mutual defense.

In "Belgium, The Showdown," Lionel sets the disconcerting scene: "For 31 agonizing months, Belgium's dapper Premier Gaston Eyskens had wrestled with his country's problems. He had set the Congo free—only to see the Congo explode into anarchy and send thousands of hapless Belgians fleeing for their lives. He had appealed to the UN for help—only to have Belgium branded as an aggressor, spurned by allies, and threatened by the Communist bloc. Then when Eyskens presented the bill for the Congo's loss to his humiliated people, half of them rose against him. Orderly little Belgium was rent with strikes that set Walloon against Fleming, Catholic against Protestant, Conservative against Socialist." Eyskens was successful in seeing to it that Russia's attempt to label Belgium as an aggressor failed at the UN. "But the pressure had been too much. As he sat in Parliament his face grew pale and he had to be helped from the chamber. Sheer exhaustion, pronounced the doctor, as the plucky 55-year-old Premier of Belgium was carried home to bed." The Congo Crisis (1960–1965) took place in the Republic of the Congo (now the Democratic Republic of the Congo). After the Congo gained its independence from Belgium, civil wars broke out. The US and the Soviet supported opposing factions (a proxy conflict). Lamentably, one hundred thousand people were killed during the crisis.

Good night, dear Lionel Durand, wherever you are!

11

Into the Eye of the Storm

Lionel Durand, Newsweek's Paris bureau chief, died Jan. 14, 1961, in Paris of a heart attack. It was a result of his being tear-gassed in Algeria, while covering riots that had erupted in the Casbah. He had gone there to interview Moslem leaders. Among his last stories were "Algeria—You-You-You-You" and "Into the Eye of the Storm." He died quietly in his sleep. Lionel Durand, who for two years was Newsweek's Paris bureau chief, had lived life to the hilt. So ended "Epitaph—A Reporter," Newsweek's account of Lionel Durand's death.

If we wish to die well, we must learn how to live well. Remembering death is not for the sake of becoming fearful but to appreciate this precious lifetime.
—Dalai Lama

L ionel valiantly covered Algeria; being on the scene cost him his life, *a tear-gas bomb exploding at his feet.* Days before his death, the *Times* reported, Lionel Durand had "told friends he had inhaled tear gas during the recent disturbance in Algeria, which he covered for his magazine, *Newsweek*. He had trouble catching his breath." President de Gaulle assured the people of Algeria that they could decide their own future. Protesting threatened loss of power, the settlers of Algeria went into the streets while the Muslims cheered for independence. It was a chaotic time of rioting and tear gas. The police fired on both contingents. After

a January 8, 1961 referendum on Algerian self-determina-
tion, Charles de Gaulle declared the results of 16.9 million
votes "to be striking": 72% of French citizens of France and
Algeria approved de Gaulle's plan to end the Algerian War
of Independence (1954–1962).

At a cabinet meeting, de Gaulle was urged to issue an official statement of appreciation for this remarkable majority. *Le Grand Charles* laconically countered: "How can
France thank France?"

Lionel's fingerprints are all over the February 8, 1960,
Newsweek special six-page section on Algeria, "France's de
Gaulle: The Final Crisis?" I read the piece, the original
Newsweek issue in hand, and found it fascinating and electric. *Newsweek* had planned to devote the magazine cover to
the boom in compact cars, but, because of the Algerian crisis, the editors rushed out a cover photo portrait taken by
the versatile Lionel "of the man whose prestige now rests on
saving the Fifth Republic—Gen. Charles de Gaulle." On January 8, 1959, de Gaulle was inaugurated as the first president
of the Fifth Republic in which executive power was increased while the National Assembly's power decreased. De
Gaulle was firm in his resolve that Algerians would have the
free choice of their fate. "That is the only policy that is worthy of France." But it wouldn't be easy, as the stakes were
high. "Four generations of Frenchmen have sweated and
toiled to make Algeria French." France was investing
$600,000,000 a year in Algeria, Africa's largest country by
area, which was rich in oil and minerals and guaranteed
shipping lanes through the Mediterranean Sea. There were
almost a million French settlers in Algeria which had a total
population of 11,277,757.

The piece specifically includes my father by name for interviews titled "Algerian Grass Roots—Confused Loyalties, Doubts, and Hopes" that he personally conducted. How did individuals with varied interests living in Algeria react to de Gaulle's crisis? To find out, *Newsweek's* "Lionel Durand interviewed an army colonel attached to a garrison in eastern Algeria, a 45-year-old settler who was a garage mechanic in Algiers, and a Moslem construction worker from Oran." I include the three interviews, shortened slightly, as an example of a reporter seeking a balanced view of different perspectives on the historic and momentous occasion that it was.

The Colonel

Where do you stand in this crisis?

I feel torn because my comrades and I have a job to do—fighting the National Liberation Front (FLN) and instead we are being drawn into a political conflict.

What do you think of the political conflict?

I see it as a fight between Frenchmen of Algeria who want to remain French and Paris politicians who don't know what they want but are prepared to give up Algeria.

Has the sense of discipline diminished in the army?

In the field, not at all. But the army has been made an important factor in the political life of the nation, not always with its consent. Some feel we must take sides.

Is the French Army obeying orders?

On the whole yes, but only up to a point. There are orders which the army would not obey. For example, we would refuse to fire on the French population—the so-called insurgents. We don't feel it is wrong for Frenchmen to demonstrate in favor of France.

If you had to choose between loyalty to General de Gaulle and keeping Algeria French, what would you do?

I frankly don't know. We have all been thinking about this. Our mission here is to keep Algeria French by fighting the FLN. Now we are told we must let the Moslems decide about independence. I do not think de Gaulle will sell out Algeria—he is a patriot and a great Frenchman. But he must take a clear-cut position in favor of keeping Algeria French.

The Settler

What do you think of the insurgent leaders?

We don't care who the leaders are. We care about the idea: we want to keep Algeria French.

Would you consider secession to keep Algeria French?

It won't come to that point. France cannot live without Algeria. And maybe we couldn't live without France.

Do you believe the settlers can impose their will on the French nation?

We are not trying to force anybody to do anything. But if Algeria ceases to be French, I might as well become a Cuban.

The Moslem

What do you think of the insurrection?

I understand little about French politics, but I think de Gaulle is trying to help us Moslems.

Are you for the FLN?

You don't know my name so I can tell you that I pay a monthly tax to the FLN collector. But I do it mostly to live in peace,

How would you vote in a free Algerian election?

Maybe for independence. But I think it's better to have good relations with France—as long as we have real equality. The settlers will never give us full equality. Maybe de Gaulle will.

****

France first occupied Algeria in 1830, and, in 1848, it was annexed into three French Departments. During the conquest, France looted, raped, and massacred entire villages. Bluntly stated by Thomas Hobbes, "War is death's feast." The insurgency and the counterinsurgency used fierce urban guerilla warfare, torture, murder, explosives, execution, abuse of women, sheer terror to intimidate and exert power over the civilians. The war was brutal and costly, destroying eight thousand villages/hamlets, creating 3,000,000 refugees. It took 500,000 French troops to finally subdue the FLN in the Battle of Algiers (1956–57). The French people had enough and lost the political will to colonize Algeria. Algerian historians say 1.5 million died in the war, while their French counterparts state that 400,000 from both sides died, horrific numbers, which probably meet in the middle. 140,000 to 152,863 FLN soldiers died; 25,600 French soldiers were killed. (Wikipedia, Algerian War) When the FLN took power, they massacred tens of thousands of *harkis*, Algerian Muslims who fought with the French.

Patrick Rotman made a four-hour 2002 documentary, *The Intimate Enemy, Violence in the Algerian War*, a "collective questioning" of human nature. Rotman interviewed dozens of veterans who admitted to having seen or practiced

torture, rape, and summary executions. "Men in their 60s—
including Jean Faure, the vice president of the French Senate—wept openly as they recounted secrets they had kept
their whole adult lives. Rotman's witnesses venture explana-
tions—racism, peer pressure, the abuse of alcohol, anger,
and the desire for revenge. Most disturbing is a former soldier's mention of 'a form of pleasure'—doing whatever you
want to a body, fulfilling your most perverse and deep desires." (*The Irish Times*, "Breaking the Silence," Lara Mer-
ton, March 16, 2002)

Martin Evans, *History Today*, July 1991, interviewed
(March to October 1989) French who helped the FLN, wanting to know, "How has this memory of the Occupation
structured their response to the Algerian war?" Was there a
connection between resistance to the Nazis and protest-fight
against colonial rule? I imagine Lionel Durand had that
burning question, mind and heart, when he went to Algeria
to cover the war. Martin writes, "Across the oral testimonies
we found that a sense of the Second World War was central
in explaining their motivations for resistance to the Algerian
war. In 1954, there were two hundred thousand Algerians
living in France. It was Algerians in France that were to fi-
nance the war. Of the French people actively involved with
the FLN the most famous were those associated with the
Jeanson network, set up in 1957. Jeanson was an intellectual
strongly associated with Jean-Paul Sartre. During the late
1940s and early 1950s, Jeanson had visited Algeria twice.
Shocked by colonialism, he contacted Algerian nationalists
and, returning to France, he wrote a number of articles
warning of the explosive situation." Aline Charby, whom
Martin interviewed, joined the Jeanson network as she "saw
the Algerian struggle against colonialism in terms of the
French Resistance. The colonial mentality was a continua-
tion of collaboration and to be done away with." Pierre

Deeschemacker was a Roman Catholic priest who was sent to Algeria in 1955. He told Martin Evans in his interview: "In the evening, I saw the body of an Algerian, which had been left on the street by the French army. This immediately reminded me of the Occupation, even if I had not seen such atrocities myself. I was deeply shocked to see that the body was still there four or five hours after the fighting. The normal human reaction would have been to take the body away. It was obvious that it had been left there to inspire fear and terror in the Algerian population." Yet illegal French resistance to the Algerian War was small. Martin Evans concludes: "We are talking about 1,000 people, 4,000 at most. Why? If the connection between the Second World War resistance and the resistance to colonialism was so obvious for them, why was it not for many more people? The answers to these questions involve consideration of the language of the majority and the strength of other influences such as colonialism, racism, patriotism and nationalism and the belief in the civilizing mission of France."

Lionel Durand (May he enjoy Eternal Consciousness, Being, and Delight and Continue with me always at invisible circular world time) was survived by his Jewish-German wife, Irène Lipszyc, born in Leipzig, 1924. Escaping from the horror of the Nazis, Irène arrived in Baltimore, July 1942; she married Lionel in 1948 in NYC. Their daughter, Barbara, was born July 16, 1952, in Neuilly, France. Sadly, on December 10, 2010, Barbara died in Hôpital de la Salpêtrière, Paris. Barbara brought two baby boys—Jérémy and Lionel—into sacred life. Now they are flourishing young men living in Belgium. I wish their mummy, Barbara, well and pray that she Enjoy Eternal Life in Peace. Irène is now 96. In March 2020 she tested positive for COVID and has lost many of her faculties. I was saddened by this news.

In 1993, nations were encouraged to sign the UN's Chemical Weapons Convention that outlawed the use of riot control agents in warfare. Being tear-gassed for some can have lasting, even lethal effects. A 2016 report published in *Annals of the New York Academy of Sciences* reports that tear gas is especially threatening if used up close. Deaths and severe injuries have been reported because of "massive-scale deployments of tear gas munitions," the report says. Tear gas (first used as a chemical weapon in WWI) can seriously affect people exposed such as at demonstrations. It might trigger an asthma attack, aggravate the respiratory system, put one at higher risk for strokes and heart attacks.

The United States is among several countries in which "tear gas use has dramatically increased in recent years." In many US cities, protesters against the May 25, 2020 horrendous killing of George Floyd have been tear-gassed just as Lionel had been when French troops suppressed protests in Algeria. The precipitating factor in Lionel's death was that a chemical weapon exploded at his feet. Lionel was tragically killed by the French colonial government, the very government Lionel Durand fought for in the French Resistance.

The George Polk Award

The Overseas Press Club of America is the nation's oldest and largest association of journalists engaged in international news. Every April, it awards the most prestigious prizes devoted exclusively to international news coverage. It was founded in 1939 by nine foreign correspondents in New York City, and has grown worldwide to nearly five hundred members, media industry leaders. The wire service reporter Carol Weld was a founding member, as were war correspondent Peggy Hull and Sigrid Schultz, the first woman to serve as Berlin bureau chief for the *Chicago Tribune*. The club seeks to maintain an international association of journalists working in the US and abroad to encourage the highest standards of professional integrity and skill in in the reporting of news and to work toward better communication and understanding among people. The club's mission is to foster excellence in news reporting, advance press freedom, and promote good fellowship among colleagues while educating a new generation of journalists.

Excerpt from the 1961 Dateline for:

The George Polk Memorial Award 1960 (presented posthumously)

AWARD: Lionel Durand, *Newsweek*'s Paris bureau chief, died Jan. 14, 1961, in Paris of a heart attack. It was a result of his being tear-gassed in Algeria, while covering riots that had erupted in the Casbah. He'd gone there to interview Moslem leaders. Among his last stories were "Algeria— You-You-You-You" and "Into the Eye of the Storm."

"He died quietly in his sleep of a heart attack." So ended "Epitaph—A Reporter," *Newsweek*'s account of Lionel Durand's death. Duran, who for two years was *Newsweek*'s Paris bureau chief, had lived life to the hilt. His interests were legion, so were his talents. Counting Picasso among his intimate friends, he was himself a painter of quality, a nimble guitarist, and fluent in six languages. He could cover a Khrushchev press conference one day and a bullfight in Spain the next.

But the big story for Durand was always politics. One of the first to predict de Gaulle's return to power, Durand was still covering a part of the de Gaulle story when he went to Africa to cover the Algerian war. He visited the Casbah to interview Moslem leaders during one of the riots and was caught in a crossfire as police tried to quell the disturbance. Though a tear-gas bomb exploded at his feet he went, coughing and sputtering, half-walking, half-running, to file his story from a cable office miles away.

He returned to the Paris bureau exhausted, the tear gas having added to the strain of the previous months. Then, Friday night, January 13, his last story written and dispatched, Lionel Durand went quietly to sleep for the last time.

12

Blessings from Out of the Blue

As soon as I saw you, I knew a grand adventure was going to happen.
—Winnie the Pooh

To adoptees. Never be afraid of searching for the truth. The joy that may await you will far outweigh the burden of your long journey.
—Diamond Mike Watson

In the middle of writing this book, blessings came to me out of the blue. I received Facebook messages from my half-sister Barbara's two sons, Lionel Changeur (b. 1972) and Jérémy Changeur (b. 1977). They said that they did not know a lot about my father Lionel, but it turned out they were full of revelatory Lionel gifts for me. At the end of this chapter, you will see a father-daughter photo of Lionel and Barbara. On the front cover is Lionel Durand's gorgeously colored portrait of Barbara as a young girl of mixed race. Speaking profoundly to me, and to others archetypically, Lionel conveys my feelings of having the same Black father as Barbara and a White mother. And finally, you can view, on the back cover a stunning gift from Pablo Ruiz Picasso himself to Lionel Durand and, by extension, to the reader. Lionel Durand did the French translation of a book, *The Private World of Pablo Picasso*, written by David Douglas Duncan. Duncan, a renowned photographer and author of *This Is War*, first met the 75-year-old Picasso while the world's greatest artist was taking a bath. Invited into the home and private studio of Pablo, Duncan had three months' access and shot over 10,000 photos, selecting three hundred of them for the book Lionel translated into French. I couldn't resist purchasing an English copy. Lionel Changeur has the books (French and English) proudly in his treasured possession. Such an affectionate and playful Lion(el) sketch by Picasso!

Lionel Changeur was named after Lionel Durand and would google his grandpa's name from time to time. Voilà! On November 28, 2020, to Lionel's surprise, the *Haitian Times* article popped up. "We just discovered that our mummy Barbara had a brother: you!"

So, with enthused expectation, we Zoomed, sharing good company and conversation as well as talking about mummy Barbara and grandparents, Irène Lipszyc (b. October 21, 1924) and Lionel Durand. We were joined by Lionel's daughter Noémie, and his wife Aurélie. Lionel and Aurélie also have an endearing six-month-old baby girl, Charlie. Jérémy was joined by his partner Chiara. They are the beaming parents of two precious young daughters, Alessia and Elisa. Jérémy works in IT and lovingly carries out his principal vocation of being an attentive partner to Chiara and a father to his two babies. Lionel, a journalist, relates that he walks modestly "in Lionel Durand's footsteps, sometimes with a heavy burden on my shoulders. He was such a splendid example of the inaccessible model." Jérémy and Lionel spoke about their appreciation for their kind mom Barbara who unfortunately suffered heart problems and hypertension. Barbara married twice, first with François Changeur and then Léon Leroy. I felt a twinge of sadness that Barbara often expressed to her family her wish that she had a brother or sister. I can now fully embrace her as my sister. We ended by exchanging warm goodbyes and a plan to Zoom again soon.

Martine responded to the news of my meeting Lionel, Jérémy, and cousin, Chantal Larouche. "Dear cousin. What terrific news! Chantal is indeed our cousin. Her grandfather Camille, yours Louis Durand and Lamercie, my great-grandmother, were siblings. Finding your nephews is a beautiful Christmas present. I am so happy Chantal got in touch with you. And that our family just got bigger. We still hope to meet you soon. Warm hugs from your family here in New York!"

Lionel had sent the link of the *Haitian Times* article to Chantal who responded: "Everyone in the family is so happy to meet a new parent. We are all excited. This is a pleasure to have all the information possible to get closer to our dear cousin, Morgan. I live in Cap-Haïtien, Haiti. My grandfather was Camille Durand. Hope to hear from you soon. *Bisous.*"

How happy I was to receive a warm, emojied answer to my email to my cousin, Josiane, Andrée's daughter, Lionel's niece! "Hello, Morgan. I feel so grateful to have another cousin, and I feel that you are already part of our family. I didn't have the happiness to know your father Lionel who was my mother Andrée's brother, my uncle. When Lionel, your dad, passed away, my mother told me that I was only five months old. Now I am sixty-five. I have two older brothers, your cousins, Joel and Alain, sons of Andrée. Joel unfortunately passed away just four months ago at the age of seventy-seven years old. Joel was a dear person; we miss him a lot. He has a son, Jean Luc, who is my nephew and my godchild. He has three children. My other brother Alain is so dear to me as well. He is alive and healthy; his wife' s name is Michelle. You know about Micheline, our dear cousin (Lionel's niece) who lives in France. She is happy to share precious souvenirs of Uncle Lionel with you. I would love to communicate with you. By WhatsApp if it is ok for you. I will be happy to send you family pictures. Chantal, Sébastien, Jérémy, and Lionel are so pleased to know about your existence. Micheline and I already feel very close to you. God bless you too, and I am in a hurry to have the confirmation that you got my message. A big hug *d'eau*, my dear cousin."

Sébastien, Josiane's son, had contacted me first via Facebook messages. "Dear Morgan, forgive me for the impromptu message as we have not met before. It appears that we are related. My apologies for the strange claim. This borders on absurdity, but I just received the most incredible article from my mother Josiane who's based in Haiti. She sends me daily online articles, and I must admit that a lot of them do go unnoticed. The *Haitian Times* article wasn't one of them! I read your amazing story about your father, Lionel Durand, my great uncle! I was born and raised in Haiti and have been living in Dubai for the past 10 years with my wife and three-year-old daughter. My mother Josiane Saurel was born to Luc Saurel and Andrée Durand, your father's sister. Andrée fled France to Haiti during the war. Sadly, she was murdered in 1992. My sincerest apologies if this message comes across as strange, and you would be right to think of it as such, but I was really compelled to reach out. My mother, Josiane, found your writing lovely, and was hoping I could help her get a closeup of the picture featured in the article. There are quite a few interesting chapters in our family history that I would love to share with you if you are interested. I am happy to write, and please know that I am not expecting to hear back from you, but secretly hoping that this message puts a smile on your face and that we are able to connect for the sake of at least helping you connect more dots! Have a wonderful weekend and in case I never hear back from you, I am glad to know that you were able to find some of those roots." Sébastien and I have spoken on the telephone and are getting to know each other through WhatsApp, email, and Facebook.

And, through WhatsApp, I texted my first cousin living in France, Micheline Durand (born 1941), Lionel's niece (daughter of Réne, Lionel's older brother) who responded in Spanish: "It gives me great pleasure that you reached out to me, and I would like very much to know you. This is a difficult time; the corona virus is making us crazy. But hopefully we will have the opportunity to share. I believe we both have a lot of wonderful things to communicate to each other. Lionel, your and Barbara's father, was not only my uncle but my godfather and idol! I met him when he was able to return to France after World War II. Merry Christmas and a Happy New Year, full of pleasant surprises. *Abrazos*."

Lionel Changeur and I, joined by John Suggs, continued our conversation about Lionel Durand, Barbara, and Irène, some of which I will share now. I was curious to know in what religion Lionel and Jérémy were raised. According to the Jewish tradition of Irène's family, her daughter Barbara and Barbara's children would be raised in the Jewish faith. Knowing Irène's family history and their personal suffering as Jews, I was surprised to discover that my nephew Lionel only learned that Irène was Jewish when he was fifteen years old. It is a sensitive subject for my nephews, and one which I am only just beginning to understand.

Having spent time researching Irène's family, we had found several books and other documents which described their life before WWII, as well as their escape from the Nazis and finding safe refuge and a new life in the USA. Leaving from Lisbon, Portugal, Irène arrived in Baltimore, Maryland, in July of 1942. She was seventeen. On the passenger manifest, her race was clearly stated as Hebrew. One of Irène's first cousins, Victor Brombert, became a highly decorated US soldier who returned to Europe to fight for their adopted homeland and for the relatives that they had left behind. Victor fought on the beaches of Normandy and in the Battle of the Bulge. The autobiography he wrote late in life is called *Trains of Thought: Paris to Omaha Beach, Memories of a Wartime Youth.* He was part of the elite intelligence unit of primarily Jewish immigrants known as "the Ritchie Boys" (Camp Ritchie, Maryland). Because they knew the German language, culture and psychology, they were assigned to every major combat unit in Europe to interrogate German prisoners of war and gather key tactical intelligence on Nazi troop movements, strength, and positions. Their important work was recognized and honored for helping save countless lives of Americans and their Allies.

Victor discovered that their aunt Anya, who had gone missing in a roundup of foreign Jews in Nice, had died in Auschwitz. I know that some survivors of the Nazis suffered Holocaust survivors' guilt (guilt without wrongdoing) which can have an untoward influence and impact for generations. Such survivors feel guilty because they lived. I do not know if that was the case for Irène, especially because she apparently lived openly as a Jew when married to Lionel. Lionel's *Newsweek* boss Ben Bradlee, a close personal friend of President John F. Kennedy, mentions Irène in his autobiography, *A Good Life: Newspapering and Other Adventures.* Bradlee affectionately described Irène (or Toto, as he called her) as a "Jew from Brooklyn." So, before she lost Lionel, Irène may have felt safe enough and secure enough to be "out" as a Jew. Perhaps that sense of security all changed for her when Lionel died, and she suddenly had to raise their eight-year-old Barbara alone. Lionel was such a remarkable man that I am certain his loss at such a young age must have hit her terribly hard.

I do not yet know why Irène was reluctant to share her Jewish heritage later in life and why she did not share it with Lionel and Jérémy when they were young boys. Hopefully, over time, more of her personal story will become known.

My nephew Lionel filled in some of the blanks: "When I was a child, I called Grandma Ninamama and that's how we call her to this day. Ninamama (Nina) kept a lot of matters secret. Since the family of my father (François Changeur) was Catholic, we were raised Catholic. My mother Barbara was not fascinated by religion. Grandma Irène spent a lot of time with me when I was a child. She was fluent in English and in German. My mother had a bachelor's degree in German, and she worked as an intern in the *Nouvel Observateur* (most prominent weekly French magazine in terms of audience and circulation) founded by Jean Daniel, who knew Lionel Durand. But my mother never became a journalist as she wanted at age nineteen to take care of her new baby. She stopped studying. My grandma was furious about this. She wanted a brighter future for Barbara, to become a famous TV journalist. She wanted her to be like Anne Sinclair, US born in 1948, who hosted one of the most popular political shows for more than 13 years on TFI, the largest European private TV channel. I was baptized and attended catechism classes. But I was a rebel. Perhaps I knew that something was wrong."

"Ninamama told me that she was Jewish when I was around 15 and somewhat uneducated. I did not know the real meaning of being Jewish. Then Grandma started to be somewhat more open about her race and explained some Judaic rites with salt, but she never avoided foods such as pork. She explained that she had to hide her Jewish identity, to get rid of her accent. I was, I could say, her confidant."

"At the age of 96, after suffering Covid-19, Nina is very fragile and silent. Fortunately, she is at peace, and I can see in her eyes that she asks herself: 'What I am doing in this world?' The Rothschild Foundation was her retirement home in Paris. That is an ironic coincidence for she basically had little consideration for Jewish traditions. But was she missing the chance to assimilate Jewish wisdom? In July 2020, we moved Grandmother next to Belgium, in the North of France, because the Rothschild Foundation retirement home in Paris was very disappointing."

Lionel continues: "Irène at last told us that she escaped from the Nazis and arrived in the US. When she met a single Lionel, he asked her: 'Are you engaged?' Irene told him no and that Lionel would not be single anymore because 'I will marry you'! At that time Irène could not take the bus with Lionel or eat in the same restaurant. Grandma suffered a lot from this segregation. When Barack Obama was elected president, it was one of her most beautiful days! The day of the revenge! She never mentioned her cousins by name. Fifteen or eighteen years ago she received a phone call from a German attorney who oversaw reparations paid for the Holocaust. The attorney mentioned one cousin (a woman) who had to share an amount of the reparation. When the check arrived, Ninamama said: 'What was all the fuss about? It was by no means a ridiculous amount of money!'"

I suspect that one of the reasons Irene and Lionel settled in France was that they would have encountered much more prejudice here in the US. I assume that France was a more open place for them to live and to raise Barbara. Mixed race marriages were illegal in some US states until 1967! There is an exquisitely poignant movie, *Loving,* which was written and directed by Jeff Nichols. With breathtaking cinematography and superb acting, it depicts the courageous Mildred and Richard Loving (Ruth Negga and Joel Edgerton) as they take their 1967 case, Loving v. Virginia, all the way to the Supreme Court, where at last the civil rights of an interracial couple to marry were affirmed. Before that, couples like Irène and Lionel were arrested in some states for the crime of being married. It was not accepted in the US and even today—though there has been definite progress—racism still exists in the US.

I can well imagine Irène's feelings when Obama became president—after everything she had lived through, side by side with Lionel. All the evidence John Suggs and I have gathered points to the fact that I was most likely relinquished and given up for adoption as a boy in the US precisely because of my mixed race. Born in 1944 to a White mother, my very existence was considered scandalous and problematic for my mother's family. They ultimately sent me away largely because of the color of my skin. So, the pain and rejection that Irène and Lionel clearly experienced here for being married to each other was also something I internalized and experienced myself for being a child of mixed race. Lionel Durand was never even told of his son's existence. Never given the option to raise his own son. And I was told that Lionel was dead even though he was very much alive until I was 16 years old. Such a wasted opportunity. And in no small part due to the prevailing racism back in the day in the US. I trust that Lionel, Irène and Barbara had it a little easier living in France. Hopefully, they did. But still the sting of racism never really goes away.

John Suggs provided Lionel and Jérémy a family tree for Irène's cousins. As previously mentioned, one of them, Victor Henri Brombert, a famous intellectual and WWII hero, wrote a book about his family's escape from France, and Sacha (Irène's brother) is featured in it. The cousins were like brothers. Irène, who escaped with them, shared the same experience. Another cousin, Marie Millner, had been an international champion bridge player before the war. Irène was an excellent bridge player in her own right. Lionel candidly admits: "Bridge partners were frightened by the idea of playing with Grandma because she hated to lose! Something in her blood. Amazing to know that."

Photo of Barbara and Lionel, courtesy of Jérémy Changeur

Conclusion

An Invincible Calm

In the midst of hate, I found there was, within me, an invincible love. In the midst of tears, I found there was, within me, an invincible smile. In the midst of chaos, I found there was, within me, an invincible calm. I realized through it all, that in the midst of winter, I found there was, within me, an invincible summer. And that makes me happy. For it says that no matter how hard the world pushes against me, within me, there is something stronger—something better pushing right back.
—Albert Camus.

Like Joseph reuniting with Jacob, you have made ready your chariot and gone up to Goshen to meet Lionel Durand, your father, and presented yourself to him and wept. Like Joseph and Jacob, our God has been with both you and Lionel since the very first.
—John F. Suggs

This concludes our story of revelation, the revealing of my sacred bond to Lionel Durand and my African ancestry, including its history of struggles for civil rights and a conversation about my own healing of adoptee trauma—with acknowledgement that all we adoptees have unique stories—and general principles of healing, both individual and collective. I attempted to answer questions posed in reaction to the *Haitian Times* article, which wanted to know the psychological and intellectual impact of a

167

reunion with my biological father, his life and his times, which included, among others, the French Resistance, Picasso, Josephine Baker, Charles de Gaulle, the Black civil rights movement, women's rights, the Vietnam War, the Algerian War for Independence, and the Cold War. "Can we truly heal personal trauma in the midst of collective trauma?" "How does reflecting on Lionel Durand and our ancestors affect us personally in contemporary times?"

I came to find my DNA home, a specialized, spiraling staircase of my ancestral identity, something I longed for starting at a young age, along with an affinity (unconsciously propelled) to support and be immersed as a reader and letter writer in the nonviolent movement of Dr. King who accompanied me in boyhood as a wise teacher and heroic model.

John F. Suggs told the incredible story of contacting my second cousin, Simone, who said to my heart's deep relief: "Morgan looks like members of our family." A ton of seeking was erased instantaneously from my psyche. And on January 15, 2019, Dr. Martin Luther King Jr. Day, as if a spiritual gift from Dr. King, John texted: *We found your father!*

We remembered stories of the 1955 Montgomery, Alabama, bus boycott, the 1957 Little Rock Central High integration of nine Black students, and Dorothy Counts Scroggins, in 1957, one of the students attempting to desegregate Harry Harding High School, Charlotte, North Carolina. I wrote about John Howard Griffin's connections to my life, as one evolving into a person of mixed racial identity and JHG's connections to Lionel's life as a fellow student at the Sorbonne and a member of the French Resistance.

I described my personal therapy, with confidence that therapy was healing for me as it can be for others. When initially told that Lionel Durand was my father, I was excited, but as if it were from a story outside me, not *my* story. I had doubts and resistance, as did a few others, until with time, loosening the tyranny of self-defeating, ingrained dissociative tendencies, I joyously accepted, embraced, and grew in my closeness to Lionel and Haitian paternal roots. I no longer am frozen in the primal wound, but it took a year-long process of integrating acceptance that I hope the reader found useful and interesting.

Then we gave some attention to accompanying collective trauma survivors, walking with the wounded, bent but unbowed. Cambodia under Pol Pot (1975–1979); the Civil War in El Salvador (1979–1992); El Mozote Massacre (December 11, 1981), El Salvador; the Acteal Massacre (December 22, 1997), Mexico; Rwandan genocide (April 7, 1994 to July 15, 1994); former gang members, former prisoners working at Homeboys Industries; Mexican working street children (some homeless) in Veracruz and Chiapas, Mexico.

We discussed how illegal adoption agencies did not have the children's best interests at heart, and how my biological mother (name withheld for privacy) struggled with being pregnant with a Black father's baby. She sought secrecy by hiring one of these illegal adoption agencies. We felt compassion for her as a pregnant out-of-wedlock mother, but doing the best she could and taking care of me for three years. I declared my disappointment in not being given to my Haitian family to raise me, and that knowledge of my African ancestry was withheld from me.

We considered forgiveness in the context of the primacy of healing. We feel free to forgive ourselves even when we cannot (or are not ready to) forgive our abuser. That requires, first of all, not wanting to pay back or wish harm to the offender. Then, with time—if it should come—to wish our abuser healing and wholeness as well.

We listened as Robert Holstein proposed a consciousness/heart-expanding spirituality of adoption. Bob talked to his children about the fear of being abandoned, of not belonging, and the desire to be accepted just as one is. He told his children and me that we were connected to, and belonged to, two families, and that we should celebrate both as much as is possible. And that at heart we all are sisters and brothers in our humanity. He spoke out against closed adoptions, sealed and tampered-with records, secret knowledge, exploitation of children in any manner, and in favor of healing, moving ahead, evolving to grow into self-confidence, friendship, and a widening circle of compassion. Robert liked to quote Fr. John Courtney Murray, SJ: "Self-understanding is the necessary condition of a sense of self-identity and self-confidence."

We presented what we know of Lionel Durand, a man of many interests and talents, a man who joined the French Resistance in 1940, twice arrested, twice escaped, hated ferociously by the Nazis because he was Black. What was it like to be in the French Resistance? We get some sense of the history-altering effort through the accounts of Jane Vialle, Eugénie Eboué, Josephine Baker, and Virginia Hall. And from Lionel Durand himself. There was an urgency for Lionel and his family to escape Nazi-controlled France. Free at last from Hitler, they arrived in New York City in 1942 where Lionel took a job with Voice of America, still part of the war effort. We shared some of the newspaper articles he would go on to write. Then, as a result of being tear-gassed in Algeria, Lionel Durand died of a heart attack on January

14, 1961. The Algerian War was looked at, and we examined if there was a link between fighting for the Resistance and fighting against colonialism in Algeria.

With delight I received FB love messages from my nephews, Lionel and Jérémy, who had located my *Haitian Times* article when googling Lionel Durand. I have been enormously blessed to connect with Haitian-born cousins and two nephews, and am getting to know them, emailing them, Zooming, Facebooking, sharing photos, planning a family reunion: feelings of pride in my Haitian blood! Immense gratitude for my cousins' and nephews' warm welcoming. Emerging is a deep veneration for Lionel Durand, honoring him as my father, biologically and spiritually. I am reborn in my mother and father's DNA, born into sacred Life. From father, I embrace how intimately I have Black roots, African roots, which likewise we all share most fundamentally. We arose from Africa, mother of our common humanity.

Discovering Lionel is a life-changing, unfolding gift, an instinctual-feeling-bodily response as well as, secondarily, an intellectual process: owning my DNA from father; genetic flashbacks connecting to ancestors; refreshed attention to Haiti, the Pearl of the Antilles; emotions percolating-gestating, crying-exulting-churning; a fuller sense of being grounded, better self-understanding, glowing in father's accomplishments; sadness in missing his company, anger at racism, consolation in an ongoing spiritual conversation and fantasy; imagining such an elegant Father, viewing the photos available, vicariously sharing his adventures, learning something about him and the me-in-him.

Meeting Lionel Durand is a continuing enrichment of my life, already happy with cherished family and friends. I wish that the story of Lionel's life, as well as those of other heroic men and women remembered, will feed our resolve to be healthier, wiser, more sensitive to social issues, kinder, more inclusive, more patient and creative people, disposed to get help when needed and to be good listeners, enjoyers and servants of this ever moving, changing life with its joys and sorrows. Within us we can find "in the midst of chaos, an invincible calm." May all beings be at Ease.

I presented myself to my father, Lionel Durand, and I wept. Now I rejoice with you, the reader, that my story of revelation and healing is being told and heard. From my heart flows abundant appreciation.

Postlude

Being Held in Love

In a meditative state, using my non-dominant left hand (possibly to be closer to the unconscious), I wrote in long hand, channeling-imagining-feeling a blessing letter from Lionel, father, to me, his son:

My Dear Morgan!
Embraces from the invisible world
Blessings to you, my firstborn, my son!
I wish you deep Ease in knowing the bond between us.
Your pride in me reflects my happiness in meeting you,
broken heart and all.
You are excited by my life, that of Lionel Durand.
I delight in you as well.
Thank God for you, for us.
Care well for your sacred vehicle,
honoring all through your living connection to
"every world."
Take yourself as your best friend, and mine too,
as we now feel each other forever,
and I love you.
Your Father, Lionel

Afterword

I first met Morgan at one of the reunions for former Jesuits in California sometime back in the early 1990s. Even though our time in the Society had never overlapped—he preceded me by over twenty years—I remember recognizing something familiar in him and liking him immediately. A friendship was quickly struck that continues to this very day. Morgan has remained that same soft-spoken, kind and gentle soul that I first met almost thirty years ago. But you will already know this, dear reader, having gotten this far in the book.

When Morgan first asked me if I would write the Afterword to his book about his father, Lionel Durand, I simply smiled and said "Of course, with pleasure." That is how it is with Morgan. He is one of those rare people who convey such a sense of joy and peace, eliciting those feelings in others, that for those of us who are lucky enough to know him and be his friend there is really nothing we wouldn't do for him. If he asks, your default response is to drop what you are doing and show up, knowing that, if he is asking, it is important, and, in the end, you are going to be the better for having done it.

That was the case for me when, back in 2014, Morgan first approached me for help on his search for his birth father. At that time, he had already, long before, successfully identified his birth mother. He was only 16 years old when he first uncovered her name by secretly using all his summer earnings from caddying at the Hillcrest Country Club in Los Angeles to hire a private detective to find her. The detective, however, only came up with her name and the name of the state agency where his adoption notice was officially filed. The detective reported that he could not find out anything else about her. Not even where she lived. And, he reported, Morgan's birth father was apparently dead. Perhaps killed in the War. But he could not even come up with a name for Morgan's father. In hindsight, we now know that this extremely limited information from the detective was due to the fact that Morgan's adoption had been both private and illegal, that his birth mother was living abroad, and that the court itself had been lied to about the death of his birth father.

Not yet knowing all of this, Morgan wrote hopefully to the state agency several times asking them to please forward an enclosed letter from him to her. They never responded back. It would be one of my sad duties to tell Morgan that I was certain that none of those letters he wrote to his mother ever reached her. Back then, it was standard operating procedure at that state agency not to contact birth mothers. And, even if they had consented to forward his letters to her, the state agency did not have a legitimate address on file for his birth mother. All correspondence had gone through the woman who had brokered the private and illegal adoption, and she was unreachable after having famously being arrested for child trafficking shortly after Morgan's placement.

Morgan never gave up, and periodically would write to the state agency—and the courts, even the Attorney General of the United States—for information. (When I eventually succeeded in accessing his complete Adoption Court File in 2015, I found one of his original unanswered letters from the 1990s sitting there.) Finally, over 45 years after he first contacted the state agency, he submitted yet another letter and this time he got a different reply. The agency had run his birth mother's name against the Social Security Administration's records of deceased persons and made the determination that she had died. And with that, they finally released additional—albeit limited—information to Morgan. This enabled him, for the very first time, to identify and reach out to her other living children—his half-siblings. Unfortunately, the startling news of Morgan's existence and, by implication, that their mother had once gotten pregnant by a man (at this point it wasn't yet known that it was by a Black man) who was not her husband and had his secret baby, was not well received by her other children. Instead of Morgan's hoped-for reunion, or even a simple acknowledgement and an exchange of medical information, no matter how awkward, the response of his half-siblings was to disavow him outright, deny that they shared the same mother, and refuse all contact.

It was shortly after this, that Morgan first learned about my expertise as an Investigative Genetic Genealogist (IGG) and reached out to me. Could I help him find out who his birth father was while also respecting his maternal half-siblings' "no contact" edict? As one is inclined to do when Morgan asks you for something, no matter how hard or difficult, without a second's hesitation, I said "Of course, with pleasure!"

So began our journey together that we are still on to this day. (As he was writing this book, we first discovered the existence of his two paternal nephews in Belgium.)

The first thing I did was review what little information that he already had. Next, I divided my efforts into two distinct areas of focus.

The first focus was to submit and analyze Morgan's DNA and compare his matches in various databases and then to reverse-engineer family trees of his best matches looking for any possible connections pointing to their joint Most Recent Common Ancestor (MRCA). Once the MRCA was found, I would then build down the MRCA's tree to identify Morgan's father. As simple as this method and tool sounds, it is, in fact, extremely difficult and time consuming. But, eventually, it will work. The truth of his parentage is there in his DNA. For, unlike one's family, the courts, the church, adoption agencies, etc., in science "DNA doesn't lie!"

The second focus would be to research his birth mother's life in great detail and reconstruct the story of her life. She was the only known person who had contact with and knew the birth father. We had to start by reconstructing her life in order to determine where and how she intersected with Morgan's birth father. This would also offer Morgan a complete family history as part of his own identity.

As we sent off Morgan's DNA for testing (which typically can take anywhere from four to eight weeks) I began researching his maternal line. Ultimately, I would track and document his maternal ancestors going back well over six or seven generations. By the time I was finished, Morgan not only possessed a whole host of original historical documents and research on his birth mother's extended family, but he may know more about the family's history and their family tree than his half-siblings do.

We discovered that Morgan's mother had been married twice. The first time in the last years before the War when she was twenty-one and still in France, where she had been born. She was married to this man when Morgan was conceived. Her second marriage occurred when Morgan was two-and-a-half, almost three-years old. At the same time as her second marriage, there were two significant events that happened in her life. Her beloved grandfather and family patriarch, with whom Morgan was being raised, died—and she became pregnant with his younger half-brother. The impact on Morgan of these simultaneous events became clear when one read the Court Adoption records. In it, the second husband made his position known that he had no desire to raise Morgan, and with his own son about to be born, wished to relinquish him for adoption. Morgan had lost his first great male family champion, his mother's grandfather in whose home he was raised for the first three years of his life. With his death, followed just a few weeks later by his mother's quick marriage to a man who did not want him, Morgan's fate was sealed.

To find his birth father, we first needed to consider the most obvious candidate and determine if Morgan was the child of her first husband. Unfortunately, this man was already dead. But our research showed that he had, likewise, remarried and we tracked down his daughter from his second marriage. We explained the situation to her and she was great. She was willing to get her DNA tested to see if her father had also been Morgan's father and thus her half-brother. The results came back negative. He wasn't Morgan's father.

Ironically the DNA tests also brought the daughter some life changing news. Based on her DNA matches, she unexpectedly learned that her father wasn't her biological father either. Born in the 1950s, she was one of the earliest sperm-donor babies in the USA. Her parents, having sought out medical assistance to get pregnant, had discovered that her father was sterile. So, they agreed to undergo treatment with

a sperm donation in order to have a family. They had in-
tended for their daughter to never know. And, but for Morgan's request that she take a DNA test, she never would have
known. Having worked with other Donor-Conceived adults
searching for their birth fathers, I was able to offer her a
great deal of support and resources including therapists, articles, books, donor-conceived support groups and so on.
She would eventually tell me that she was glad that she finally knew the truth. So many things made sense to her now.
DNA doesn't lie.

With our newfound knowledge that his birth mother's
first husband had been sterile throughout their marriage, it
helped explain how she would come to have an unplanned
pregnancy. She may have mistakenly thought that it was she
who could not get pregnant.

Our research further revealed that, while she was pregnant with Morgan, his birth mother was living in London
working for the US Office of War Information (OWI) as
part of the buildup to the Normandy invasion of June 6,
1944. We learned that she had been relieved of duty and had
returned to New York aboard a troop carrier in August,
1944 six months pregnant with Morgan. It was at this junc-
ture that she first had contact with Alice Satterthwaite, the
baby trafficker who would come to have such an outsized
influence on Morgan's young life. At the time, Alice was
working with the Red Cross and the US Army assisting pregnant, unmarried Army and Red Cross Nurses to conceal
their pregnancies and quietly relinquish their babies for
adoption. Morgan's birth mother ended up in Alice's maternity home (an apartment in NYC) in the last stages of her
pregnancy. But here was where his birth mother did something quite unusual. She did not relinquish her baby to Alice
when he was born. She kept him and, with her grandfather

and other family members, raised him until he was finally handed over to Alice a day before his third birthday. Alice would eventually escape her child trafficking charges with just a slap on the wrist because of her war work with the Army and the Red Cross. In essence, she knew too much that could have embarrassed both the Army and the Red Cross.

We are faced with the realization that in February 1944, the month Morgan was conceived, London was teeming with Allied soldiers. There were three million American soldiers alone stationed in Britain between 1942–1945. Morgan's father could have literally been any one of them, or soldiers from a whole host of different countries traveling through London. So, who was he?

Because Morgan's birth mother had been born in France, and the Free French forces and the government-in-exile under de Gaulle were stationed in London at the time, and because Morgan's first language had been French, we initially spent our time looking towards France for his father. In that frame of mind, we noted that his mother had given Morgan a very distinct French first and middle name which we suspected might be clues. At one point, early on, we found a Frenchman with those exact names—but transposed! Perhaps she had hid a clue and transposed his father's name. This man was the right age and so on. Might he have been Morgan's father? We carefully approached the man's surviving children in France and gently suggested the possibility. To their everlasting credit, they immediately embraced the possibility and consented to a DNA test. The primary challenge though was that France has very strict laws prohibiting the general usage of DNA tests. It actually requires a court order to take a DNA test in France. So, for them to assist us in our search and not violate the law in

France, one of them graciously offered to take the test while
he would be on an already-scheduled vacation in Miami,
Florida. And that is exactly what happened. Morgan and I
excitedly flew to Miami and met him. He took the DNA test.
For almost two months, we all eagerly waited for the test
results to come back. Sadly, when they did come back the
results showed that his father was not Morgan's father. DNA
does not lie.

It was after this whole huge effort failed that I went back,
once again, to the drawing board. What was I missing in
Morgan's DNA? What wasn't I seeing? And then it dawned
on me. On the periphery of all his DNA matches were a very
small number of people who were showing historical familial ties to Haiti. Their numbers were quite small and barely
made a dent. I now realized that this was because there are
very few people from Haiti doing DNA testing, and thus
there are very few Haitians in the database from which to
compare. So, because they were small numbers, most likely
they were not a representative reflection of what I was looking for.

To test my hypothesis, I did another deep dive into Morgan's DNA results, and this time there it was. I saw it. Hiding
in plain sight. Something I had looked at numerous times
before but never fully registered when I was busy looking for
his father in France. Morgan's DNA ethnicity result covered
a total of 16 distinct regions of the world. The largest were
Russia, Eastern Europe and Western Europe. There was one
outlier region at 13 %, Benin & Togo, which I had previously
noted but largely ignored. Until now. I then looked at four
other regions that I had also previously noted but largely ignored because they clocked in between only 1% to 3% each.
They were Nigeria, Ivory Coast & Ghana, Senegal and Mali.
All in Africa, and all taken together they added up to 21% of

Morgan's DNA. Now, we know that each person's four grandparents represent between 20% to 25% of one's DNA. This means that with this type of combination it was entirely possible for one of Morgan's grandparents to be 100% Black African. Or two of them to be some mixed combination including Black African.

Since we knew who Morgan's birth mother was, and we knew her European and Russian ancestry, this meant that his Black African DNA could only come from Morgan's birth father, who clearly wasn't French. He was most likely a French-speaking Black Haitian. This certainly explained why Morgan was getting those handful of Haitian matches. I really should have seen this sooner. But in all the years that we had been searching, Morgan had never broached that possibility with me. I had just wrongly assumed that his father was White—even when the DNA data disputing it was right there for me to see. This speaks volumes about the power of unconscious racial bias. I know to always follow the DNA wherever it leads. And I am embarrassed to admit that I had not done it here with my friend Morgan. I had been operating with false assumptions from the very first.

His birth mother's family was quite socially prominent. Only a few weeks after she returned from London in 1944, a major east coast newspaper did a profile on her and her family. It highlighted not only her most recent work with the OWI but detailed the illustrious war records in World War I of her father, her uncle, and her grandfather, who was an eminent surgeon. But it wasn't just his birth mother's efforts to conceal his mixed heritage. Morgan's adoptive father had also insisted that Morgan was White and raised him to be White. The efforts his birth mother and his adoptive father had exerted to keep his Black origins secret over seventy-five years ago were still alive and active right here in the present, with Morgan and me both falling victim to it. DNA doesn't lie, but one's unconscious racial bias can and most certainly does lie.

So, I started to reverse-engineer these Haitian match-trees—looking for a Most Recent Common Ancestor. The existing trees were meager and only went out a few generations, yet I could tell that they had connections with each other by the locations cited and that they all shared DNA amongst themselves. The elusive answer of his father's identity was going to be found in Haiti, of that I was certain.

Having done my analysis, it was time to share the news with Morgan. He had been so hopeful that his father had been the Frenchman with the transposed name. The family had welcomed him with such warmth. I don't know who was more disappointed when the results came back negative—them or him. He still remains in contact with them and keeps them in his prayers. I remember calling Morgan and gently telling him the news: "Morgan, Your DNA is showing us that your Dad was not French. He was actually Black, or at least of mixed race. Most likely he was Haitian."

As Morgan writes so eloquently in this book, our conversation that day was the first time in his long life that he allowed himself to consciously believe the truth: that his father was Black. Unconsciously, as this book so powerfully attests, it had always been there. But this was the moment when it finally became conscious.

Thank you, Morgan, for letting me share that sacred moment with you.

And so, now we began the next and final phase of our journey together. We were getting closer to finding Lionel Durand.

We knew that his birth mother had been working in the Office of War Information (OWI) both in New York and in London. We knew that she left London in August 1944. But when did she arrive? Was she in London or New York in February 1944, when Morgan was conceived? We knew how important that one piece of information was to our ever identifying his birth father. In an attempt to lock down, once and for all, the exact location of Morgan's birth mother in February 1944, I went and spent a week ensconced in the US National Archives outside Washington, DC.

The National Archives house millions and millions of original documents and records covering the entire two and half centuries that the USA has been in existence. All of the records created by the OWI are sitting right there in the archives, from their reports and policy memos to personnel records and everything in between. If there exists a record of the whereabouts of Morgan's birth mother in February 1944, it will be here. And sure enough, over the next several days, I began to find several clues. I found her cited, under her married name with her first husband, in an August 1944 London Office Staff Report as having left for the NY Office "for health reasons and personal emergencies."

As the days continued, I finally found her mentioned in a report from the summer of 1944 regarding the launch of a new radio news program. The report verified that she and several others had only arrived and begun work on the program in the late spring of 1944, after being sent from New York. She was in New York in February 1944! In the report, the head of the program then proceeded to complain

strongly about her, along with a few others: their total lack
of experience and training for the program. The whole thing
was taking him longer than originally anticipated, he grum-
bled, because he was having to train them from scratch. He
pointedly asked the New York office to please, in the future,
do a better job of screening candidates before sending them
over. In an unexpected way, the fact that she was in over her
head, having arrived without the proper experience or training and also pregnant, served to greatly humanize her for
Morgan and myself. She was young and inexperienced, dealing with a tough and demanding boss in wartime London
amidst the German V-1 Flying Bomb attacks, facing an unplanned pregnancy by a Black man who was back in New
York.

A glimpse into her personal situation in London that
spring and summer of 1944 is given by reading Lucy Bland's
2019 book, *Britain's 'Brown Babies'*. In it she documents the
impact and long-term social challenges that resulted when
approximately 240,000 Black American service members
were stationed in Britain between 1942 and 1945. An estimated two thousand children were born as a result of relationships that were formed by them with British women.
These mixed-race children were routinely stigmatized and
called "half-castes" by the British, and "Brown Babies" by
the American Black press.

Bland's research shows that in race and class-conscious
Britain, the children who were raised by their birth mothers
and/or their grandparents fared the best overall, but nevertheless they also experienced the social stigma and discrimination. For those children who were not raised by their
birth mothers or their grandparents, the ongoing social
stigma and discrimination they faced made it almost impossible for them to be adopted. The majority of them, sadly,

were left to be brought up in institutional settings. Making them "bastards," and racially discriminating against each of these children, was first established by the US military's policy of refusing to allow Black service members permission to marry the White mothers of their babies. This was in stark contrast to the estimated one hundred thousand British WW II "GI War Brides" of White service members who were allowed not only to marry, but also to emigrate to the United States with their children. Bland's work gives us probably the most realistic snapshot of what was facing Morgan and his birth mother that summer of 1944 in London.

In retrospect, the fact that his birth mother and her grandfather and extended family raised Morgan for the critical first three years of his life certainly gave him the stability and ability to reach key developmental markers and milestones. But it would appear that the same difficulty in adopting one of these children in Britain was present in the United States at the time. One only has to consider the fact that the "price" Morgan's adoptive parents demanded in exchange for adopting a mixed-race child was the complete erasure of his mixed heritage, his French language, his identity. They would steadfastly raise him to be White in a White family. That was the bargain that they struck in adopting him. Of course, Morgan was never consulted or given a choice in this bargain.

Our search for Morgan's father continued apace. Because the numbers of Haitians in the DNA testing databases continue to remain small, I never told Morgan this (before now) but I was very concerned that I would not find his birth father while Morgan was still alive. With each passing birthday for Morgan, it gnawed at me.

Then one day, I saw a new match in the database, a woman who shared 205 cM with Morgan, indicating that she was between a second and a third cousin of his on his father's side. (In genetics, a centimorgan—abbreviated cM—is a unit for measuring genetic linkage.) But who was she? She had no family trees attached to her account. It appeared that her account was in her own name and not managed by anyone else. She had a very common Haitian name. She had only tested in just one database—AncestryDNA. She almost never logged into her account. I sent her direct messages through the Ancestry platform asking her to contact me. She never responded. I searched and searched for her to no avail. Who was she?

Every time I would login to Morgan's account there she would be. Highest paternal match. No response and no changes.

I continued to search for her. One day I found yet another woman with the exact same name. This time she was living in New York City. She was around the right age. She was living with her daughter and her family. I had made so many attempts before but who knows? Maybe this was her?

I call her on a Saturday afternoon. She picks up. I gently explain who I am and why I am calling. I ask her if she ever took a DNA test with AncestryDNA? "Yes," she said.

My heart stops.

She says that her son-in-law had given it to her a while ago and she had taken it.

It is her!!!! It is her DNA!!

There are tears in my eyes as I write this.

I explain that I have been trying to reach her via the site.

"Oh, I never go on there. My son-in-law handles it."

I start to gush and I tell her about Morgan and how she is his closest match. Starting to feel light-headed, I slip and blurt out that he never has had anyone match him closer to his father. That he is adopted and doesn't know his family. (The first rule in this type of call is to never lead with the fact that your client is adopted. It is too risky. You can never predict how people will react to that information. Ugh! What a rookie mistake! And I know better!)

She hands the phone over to her daughter where I get a second chance to explain the purpose of my call.

She listens politely for a minute or two and then says she isn't interested and hangs up.

I stare at my phone. Both still excited and a little bit in shock. We found her! At long last, we found her! After all these years. And Morgan is still alive! I start to cry tears of joy and I just lose it.

Morgan has already related the story earlier in the book about how I went to their home early the next morning and spoke to his cousin in person. That Sunday was the Feast of the Epiphany. How utterly fitting.

With the names of her four grandparents, I was quickly able to build out the trees and identify their shared Most Recent Common Ancestor (MRCA). And a few days later I found him!! I found Lionel Durand, Morgan's father! He and Morgan's birth mother were colleagues working in the same OWI office in New York City. Lionel was on the Voice of America Desk.

Later, I would return to the National Archives and pull Lionel's records. I would find an original FBI letter signed by J. Edgar Hoover himself. It gave details of one of Lionel's encounters with the Nazis while in France. Despite the color of his skin, he was an active part of the French Resistance having been captured by the Gestapo twice and escaped twice. He was young, dashing, brave, sophisticated, tall, handsome and smart. It is easy to see how Morgan's birth mother would fall for him.

Luckily for all of us, Morgan has, at long last, found his way home and, in the doing, has found his beloved father Lionel Durand quietly abiding and waiting patiently for his son. Morgan has undertaken a Hero's Journey of healing, self-discovery and identity, and returns to us with this gift of his father's life—a life that calls out to be remembered and shared.

John F. Suggs
Westport, Connecticut
January 30, 2021
jsuggs@family-orchard.com

Appendix 1

Original *Haitian Times* "First Person" Article

The author's original article was published on August 16, 2019 in *The Haitian Times*, founded in 1999 as a weekly English language digital newspaper based in Brooklyn, NY. The newspaper is widely regarded as the most authoritative voice for the Haitian Diaspora.

FIRST PERSON—A Father and Son Reunion

By Morgan Zo Callahan

I had no idea who my father was for the first 74 years of my life. Given up for adoption, all I knew was what the adoption records stated: that my father had died before I was born.

I often wondered who he was. How did he die? Had he even known he was going to be a father? Since I was born in 1944, was he a soldier? Did he die in the war? Was his death the reason I was put up for adoption?

My adoption papers, offering no clues, merely stated about me, Morgan Zo Callahan as a child:

"The boy is a dark-complexioned child, thin and wiry with curly brown hair and large somewhat solemn eyes. On . . . the day before his third birthday, the child . . . was brought to the house of adoptive parents. Nothing is known of this child's life up to this date."

Seeking to find the answers that have eluded me all my life, I submitted my DNA to Ancestry.com. When the results came back, I got my first clue: the DNA showed that my father was of African heritage and that my paternal DNA matches in the database were all Haitians. Unfortunately, because so few Haitians have submitted their DNA for testing, the matches I had were few and only distantly related.

So, I hired a professional genetic genealogist, John F. Suggs, to help me in my search. It was from him that I finally learned who my father was: Lionel Durand, an eminent Haitian journalist. Sadly, I also learned that my father had been alive and well for the first 17 years of my life but had never known of my existence.

Lionel Durand had been denied his right to know me—and I him—and to be named as my father on my birth and adoption documents.

So, who was my father?

I learned that Lionel studied at the Sorbonne, Heidelberg, and Oxford, and spoke French, English, German, Russian, Spanish, and Italian. Lionel's father, Louis Durand (b. 1863), was a prewar Haitian ambassador to France. The Durand family found themselves trapped in France when the Germans invaded in 1940.

****

The *New York Times* recounted that Lionel Durand was a former member of the French Resistance who was "twice arrested by the Gestapo and twice escaped." Lionel faced the added difficulties for Blacks fighting in the French Resistance. Former resistance fighter, Philippe de Vomécourt wrote in 1961: "For coloured men in France, a 'safe house' or false identity papers were an impossibility. To be a coloured man in a district occupied by the Germans was to know that death was near. The Germans had a pathological fear and hatred of coloured men." Yet, in spite of this, Lionel nevertheless joined and fought in the Resistance.

As part of a wartime special investigation by the FBI, a report, filed under the signature of J. Edgar Hoover, noted that Louis Durand, the Haitian Consul in La Havre France, had returned to his home on July 16, 1941 and encountered four German soldiers who demanded his passports and those of his family. The soldiers confiscated the following: diplomatic passports and passports of Durand's family; exequatur and act of nomination by Haitian Government; marriage certificate of Durand's son, Lionel; official and private letters; all consular seals; blank passports; and notes belonging to Durand's son and a photograph. They were now without any identification papers to protect them in occupied France.

In the summer of 1942, the family finally successfully fled France for NYC, where Lionel was appointed director of Voice of America's French section regularly broadcasting to the peoples of occupied France.

✻✻✻✻✻✻✻✻

He knew Paris as well as he knew the keyboard of his battered typewriter, and there was never an American visitor who wanted a glass of wine, or a wise briefing on French politics,

or a gay laugh in a bistro, who did not get it freely from him.
This was Lionel Durand.
—*Haiti Sun,* January 29, 1961

Lionel returned to France in 1956 and eventually joined
Newsweek. "As a former member of the Resistance he knew
most of the major figures of that heroic era up to and including President de Gaulle."

Lionel, a painter himself, must have been so energized
being friends with Pablo Picasso. When *Newsweek* did a picture story on Picasso's London exhibition, Pablo supplied
his own captions for Lionel's photographs. "I did this," explained Picasso, "out of friendship for Lionel."

In 1957, Durand was among the first reporters from the
West to talk to Nikita S. Khrushchev. Lionel was covering
the four-day and four-night celebration of Bolshevism's
40th anniversary. Long-winded NSK, got things rolling with
a three-hour speech to 17,000 Communists from 61 nations.
"His sputniks launched and his rule secure, Nikita S.
Khrushchev was rattling rockets, and talking peace on Soviet
terms."

After a January 8, 1961 referendum on Algerian self-de-
termination, Charles de Gaulle declared the results of 16.9
million votes "to be striking." 72% of French citizens of
France and Algeria approved De Gaulle's plan to end the Algerian War of Independence (1954-1962). The settlers of Algiers went into the streets to protest while the Muslims
cheered for independence. The police fired on both contingents. 1.5 million died in the war say Algerian historians
while their French counterparts say four hundred thousand
from both sides died, horrific numbers.

Covering Algiers cost Lionel his life. Lionel died from a heart attack on January 14, 1961, a result of being tear-gassed in Algeria.

Lionel Durand was survived by his Jewish-German wife, Irène Lipszyc, born in Leipzig,1924. Escaping from the horror of the Nazis, Irène arrived in Baltimore, July 1942; she married Lionel in 1948. Their daughter, Barbara, was born July 16, 1952, in Neuilly, France. Sadly, Barbara died in Hôpital de la Salpêtrière, Paris. Lionel, his wife and daughter all died without ever knowing about me—his son.

My new-found father, Lionel Durand, has been an enrichment of my life, already happy with cherished family and friends. Discovering Lionel is being reborn in my father's DNA, connecting to Haiti and Africa. I have been blessed to meet Haitian born cousins; feelings of pride in my Haitian blood and in the life of a remarkable Haitian reporter: war hero, Lionel Durand.

Appendix 2

Reactions to the *Haitian Times* Article

(*The Haitian Times* is the largest online newspaper for the Haitian Diaspora.)

From my cousin's daughter: "I love seeing your pictures. . . . You look so much like my uncles and cousins. I would love to meet you, and even more, for you and my mom to meet. Thank you for allowing us to be a part of this. I have always been interested in my genealogy. This gift you gave me has had me reaching out to the outer branches of cousins I barely know. I am learning all those little stories that make us who we are. I feel transformed. We all enjoyed this process, like some force was pushing us together to help you find your way to us. You are one of us. You are our cousin, and we are so blessed to have found you."

"I thank John and God for bringing you, our long-lost cousin, back to us. Something tells me your father and my great-grandmother (she was very pious) had a lot to do with it as well. I told John that I hope this year brings together our and other families who have been displaced all over the world. I am wishing you a very Happy New Year! Health, peace and love!"

"Hello! My brother Lionel Changeur and I, Jérémy Changeur, are the sons of Barbara Durand mentioned in the *Haitian Times* article. Would it be possible to get in touch with Mr. Durand's child, the author, who actually is our uncle?"

"I just discovered that my mummy had a brother: you! I read the article in the *Haitian Times*. I am Lionel Changeur, the grandson of Lionel Durand and son of Barbara who died unfortunately in 2010. So, you are my uncle!"

"I wouldn't say I and my brother know a lot about our grandfather Lionel. In your article we read things we didn't know about the Resistance period. I guess it was an epic exercise to find out who your real father was. Can't wait to see you on Zoom."

"My sincerest apologies if this message comes across as strange, and you would be right to think of it as such, but I was really compelled to reach out as soon as I read your article. My mother shared this article that she found lovely, and was hoping I could help her get a closeup of the picture featured in the article. Lionel was my great uncle. There are quite a few interesting chapters in our family history that I would love to share with you if you are interested. I am happy to write, and please know that I am not expecting to hear back from you, but secretly hoping that this message puts a smile on your face and that we are able to connect for the sake of at least helping you connect more dots! Have a wonderful weekend and in case I never hear back from you, I am glad to know that you were able to find some of those roots."

"Let me start with the obvious. You are a rich man, Morgan, for having such a great friend in John. Thank you both for sharing this treasure trove with us. I am carefully reading every single article of Lionel Durand and staring at each picture with great care. Those are going to keep me up for a while and for that I'm delighted. Lionel's legacy certainly deserves nothing less than my full attention. Your father, Lionel Durand, was an impressive man, and I am beaming with pride to have had such an accomplished great uncle. What a story! We will talk on the phone soon. I live in Dubai."

"Everyone in the family is so happy to meet a new parent. We are all excited. This is a pleasure to have all the information possible to get closer to our dear cousin, Morgan. I live in Cap-Haïtien, Haiti. My grandfather was Camille Durand. Hope to hear from you soon. *Bisous.*"

"Many thanks. It brings me such joy to communicate with you, and I hope to get to know you. Lionel, your and Barbara's father, was not only my uncle, but also my godfather and idol. I knew him when he returned to France after World War II."

"Thank you, John Suggs, for helping Morgan fill in the blanks about his adoptive origin and the identity of his father. Hoping someday to connect with the biological family of my mother, adopted as a baby . . . maybe a distant cousin . . . through the miracle of modern genetics. We all want to know where we came from."

"He was an amazing man. I get it that you are proud of him. He would be proud of you as well. Wonderful! We looked at the pictures you sent of your dad and looked at pictures of you from a recent California visit, and we totally see the resemblance!"

"Great autobiography! Great ancestry! It's good to know about your biological father. How much greater would it be to know your spiritual Father?! To know Him is to be Him. I and my Father are One. Blessings from India."

"I finally got to read your article. Very impressive. I'm so sorry you never got to meet your father and the rest of the family. Did you communicate with Skip Gates? You could be on TV! That was some pretty good genealogy research. Henry Louis "Skip" Gates is the Harvard professor who hosts the 'finding your roots' program on public TV. Google him. I was just kidding because you already did most of what the show does. Based on your genes you should be a great linguist, spy, counter-revolutionary, and writer."

"Thinking of you at Christmas. Thank you for sharing the thrilling story of your father. It reads like a novel! Hope we can have lunch again after Covid passes. Take care! With affection."

"Thanks so much for sharing the final outcome of your journey. How wonderful to finally meet your father and see your connection. He was an extremely accomplished man and you reflect that. I am deeply touched."

"How happy I am for you. What a marvel to know your father's background. As a psychologist in Xalapa, Mexico, I attend to some adoptees, and they most often want to know about their origins, mother and father, and the reasons for their adoption. Your story is so emotional for me."

"Your riveting story is so powerful. Adopted, I am in the process of having my DNA analyzed and you've given me some energy for my own search."

"I am so moved to hear the story of your father! Even from high school days, I sensed your need to know about him. What a fascinating man—and handsome to boot.

Really inspiring and worthy of a much longer article or book than the fine piece you wrote for *The Haitian Times*. Much love."

"I cannot say I understand your emotional state at your discovery. But I can easily understand a child's mixed sadness and happiness when lost in the crowd then finding parents again after some painful, anxious search. It's a sense of belonging, going home, being held by your parents again, and finally, at last peace of mind again. No wonder you have such unusual qualities, handed down by a distinguished father and carried inside you silently for decades. Now let us celebrate your important discoveries."

"Thank you for your account of finding your birth father. I found it mesmerizing to follow. I'm happy that the thread of karma conspired to reveal all of this to you even if it was not possible to meet your father in this life. He would have no doubt been delighted to discover his son."

"Wow! You have such a powerful story that gives me an incredible energy."

"I had no idea you were adopted, but I have been thinking lately quite a bit about the impact our ancestors have on our own life trajectory and seemingly inexplicable impulses. No doubt you felt the presence of your biological parents even without knowing their names or circumstances. Sending you love from Berlin."

"How wonder-filled your days must be as you have discovered your amazing father! I do rejoice with you as you savor all these realities that have come your way. And to think that you can trace strands in you that extend all the way back to your father, and now you can see from him who you are and where you can go and who you can become yet because of what and who is within you. No matter how late in life, it is real and grace-filled to say the least (est). Thank you for sharing all of this in such an elegant fashion."

"I am so touched by your remarkable account of your amazing father. The introduction hooked me into reading the whole story. He left an amazing legacy from Haiti to France, Germany, Africa (Algeria), America. No wonder why the books/articles you have been writing and sense of helping others seem to be in the blood of your biological father. I hope you will meet your Haitian cousins."

"I share your joy at discovering the remarkably courageous and gifted man your father was and is. You must treasure the reality that your mother treasured the man he was by becoming intimately connected to him, which wonder of wonders, brought the gift of you to all of us, your friends, and to all those you have touched in your unique, gentle loving way!"

"Oh wow! That is such wonderful news. I know it's been a very long and difficult search so I'm happy you were able to find some information about your biological father. He sounds like an interesting man that led an eventful life. I'm sure you're overwhelmed by a mix of emotions. I hope this will bring you some peace and joy in learning more about your father. We cherish this moment with you!"

"I bet your dad was compassionate, good natured, and a very good basketball player."

"This is wonderful news. You finally have closure. I feel blessed to have known and brought up by my dad who died at 52."

"Such nice news here in France to wake up to. I feel so happy for you, and my children are so pleased. It's incredible. I'm imagining how happy you must feel."

"This is a tremendous story. It's really a book."

"Appreciate your sharing this so important moment of your life. We are happy you found an answer to your quest. We can easily imagine all the happiness in your family as this is so incredible."

"I'm deeply flattered you chose to include me in the sending of your article. As one whose mongrel heritage and tangled DNA makes yours akin to royalty, an impressive one. Well done. Love and happiness to us all."

"You, your mom and your dad are so entwined, blessed, and fortunate to be reconnected."

"Thanks so much for sharing this incredible news of your father and his heroic life. It will make a best seller if you publish it!"

"Great stuff. Reading in the Singapore airport. Will digest and celebrate with you as the time zones adjust."

"Wow. Nice to have some of that information isn't it? To fill in the gaps."

"Fine looking man, Morgan, but for all of his accomplishments, it's too bad he never knew that his best one was to have you as a son."

"Remarkable news about your father. I can see you in your father's face. You are half Haitian! How interesting and exotic is that!"

"What a wonderful photo of Lionel. It presents him as a stunning, elegant, sensitive, mesmerizing person, so striking! It is sad that he never knew you in person."

"What a pleasant surprise to read this morning in Rwanda. I am so touched by this incredible information that appeals to my Rwandan sensibilities. Very touching, makes me feel blessed to be your friend."

"I can't imagine how you must feel finding out about your biological father. Like yourself I was impressed at the quality of the man. No wonder you are how you are. Great roots! Blessings to you, dear heart."

"What an encouraging and fulfilling confirmation of your search for your biological father, distinguished in his professional career despite its being cut short. Your own life-long personal quest to help those less fortunate reflects your dad's DNA. Congratulations!"

"Amazing father, good news. This is really good news. This is great news."

"Read your article and all I can say is WOW! I'm delighted and brokenhearted at the same time. I'm thrilled that you reconnected to your father and you are blessed to know your history—and what an amazing and beautiful one it is!"

"That's an incredible story. Some genes you've got, my friend!"

"Wow! This is totally awesome. Congrats! I vote this the best news I've had in a while."

"I am deeply moved by your story. I will read it again because there's so much mystery and miracle in it. You are a blessed child of God whom I'm lucky enough to have met!"

"Darling, what a wonderful story and it's true! May I share with a dear friend? He recently found out that his dad fathered an out of wedlock child. Much love."

"What a talented journalist Lionel Durand was. You must be excited and proud to have finally discovered your impressive roots. Your father was an amazing man who lived a high-profile life. What an accomplishment to have studied at three prestigious universities and to have mastered six languages. An excellent newsman and a good man indeed! Now I know where you got your talent for foreign languages. No wonder you are an accomplished writer and a great person. I am so happy for you to finally have uncovered your paternal roots and to have found so much of which you should be proud, including certainly your Black blood. So glad you have connected with your Haitian cousins. You must be very proud of your heritage!"

"Thanks for sharing this beautiful discovery, amazing story of your roots. I must express the feelings that rise up in me. You are the son of a truly outstanding man, Lionel Durand—his aliveness, passion, and talents were truly unusual—in his thirst for life, he lived a fuller life in fewer years than most live in a longer span. And then your mother. I love how you are now filled with gratitude at their love, however brief, that gave you life. Yes, sad that you never connected with either of them (when you might have, given other circumstances) but they are as alive for you now as any of our departed loved ones are for us who have lost beloved parents. So good you are connected to Haitian cousins—with whom you share a rich heritage—from Africa to the

Caribbean. This discovery has certainly tempered, it seems, some of the unease you often felt about your unknown origins. Thanks to God (and John Suggs)."

"My God, what a story!! Thanks for including me in the shared circle but it obviously deserves the widest possible circulation when the time is ripe! It's a wonderful story, so human, so exciting, so tragic, so compelling and inspiring, so gratifying that you finally discovered the truth of your existence. It vastly transcends the normal everyday adoption scenario (although there is probably no 'normal' adoption). So many questions/possibilities: What if you had known this much earlier? Would it have changed your early life? Your self-confidence? Do you publish some more for a wider audience? This is an absolutely thrilling slice of life. And you're part of it!"

"Oh my, what a fascinating story! My first cousin did our research on heritage, and we are of French heritage on my mother's side. My cousin went way back to the 1700s. It's fascinating but he has not yet published the research. My paternal grandmother was a native or descendant of the Indigenous Carib people. I'm from a small island (240 square miles) in the Caribbean, Saint Lucia, which is the birthplace of two Nobel laureates, the highest per capita of the awards in the world. I spent the first 19 years of my life in Saint Lucia. My father's second wife was a Haitian, but I've never visited that country. I have visited the Dominican Republic many times on vacation."

"Thanks so much for your account of your genealogical search for your biological roots. Your father was clearly immensely gifted, and I was moved by your tribute to your mother and father for giving you life. I remember Father Armand Nigro's reflection on his parents having 'loved him into existence.' Your parents would certainly have been proud of you."

"Greetings from Veracruz, Mexico. I see that your long search for your biological parents has borne fruit. God has helped you with people who have assisted you find and confirm the identity of your father. It gives me such pleasure to know how proud of your father you are. Congratulations."

"I note that your father had curly hair, was handsome, tall, and with the same eyebrows as you! What a gift you have been given!"

"I cannot tell you how much I enjoyed your wonderful biography of your father. I think it is worthy of a longer article and would make a spectacular movie. You put the story (though I was left wanting more) together so beautifully, an amazing story that moved me to tears. Truly fascinating. Helped me reflect on my own biological roots. You should be very proud."

"Fascinating account of your father's bloodline and the unexpected twists along the way. It's the irreducibility of the human family that stands out for me. Not just the biological seamlessness of the human interconnectedness, but the inseparable effects history plays in shaping who we are and where we come from. It's strange to consider that any transformation of either human history or that of the individual must begin with the ancient admonition expressed in the *Yoga Vasistha,* that 'This Maya (play of the world) is utterly unfathomable.' At first this sounds like another Eastern argument for escapism from the world, but when entered into more deeply, it proves to be a revelation of the inherent Unity of all beings and worlds. It can't be figured out because *It* can never be sliced into pieces nor can the whole be 'objectively' viewed from any position apart."

"I was flattered, if not honored, to receive your extremely interesting story. You did right by all the players (including John Suggs) and even the times of your father's career. Your narrative means a lot to me."

"You are Lionel's continuing story of goodness and truth! Blessings."

"What a wonderful gift you have received in meeting your father and knowing what a fine and talented man he was. It showed me that the old saying is true, an apple does not fall far from its tree, in this case I see so much of you in your father. I was moved to reflect on my own familial roots which was beneficial to me."

"So good hearing about your search for your father and your remarkable finds. What a man! He would have been proud of you and your dedicated life."

"What news, what joy for you and all of us. Your friend and my dear departed husband would have taken you to Haiti to celebrate and savor the knowing, the relief and deep completion you must be experiencing. You must have so many questions which cannot be answered but knowing that your father was such a fine person you can imagine whatever you wish. I looked and saw his beautiful face. You look like him to me! Already you are his son, a writer. Thrilling news."

"The story of your father is breathtaking. What a heroic man—and what a gift."

"Your unquenchable thirst for the truth behind your origins has, at long last, brought you peace and satisfaction of knowing who you are and where you come from."

"I'm blown away. Your story is worthy of a book. What an adventure!"

"You are a gem for sharing your account and reflections of finding Lionel Durand. Of course, the story resonates with me because of my own situation in losing my mother at age five and then finding her 30 years later. Goodness. We can only guess why such things happen, but we must always find the means and reasons to celebrate that they did, tough as it can be."

"An extraordinary personal story. What a journey too, to find your true place in life. You are a gift to all of us privileged to be born."

"Grateful you would share this memoir of your dad. I am incredibly grateful and so overwhelmed by your life-long search for your father. It must have been soul-rending to have gone through that lack of knowledge for so long. But how very marvelous and wonderful and INSPIRING to find you had such a parent. What a man! I am so sorry he didn't know of your birth; what a void, abyss, gap for you—for so super long a time, too! But you have much to rejoice about and what a great man to find now as your progenitor and, indeed, albeit you are no longer a kid, a true role model. I loved the whole story of your search—and your find! I felt for you every step of the way. You are truly your father's son! Blessings and thanks for sharing this significant, meaningful epoch of your life with me. Proud to have taught you in my very first class at Loyola High School. Peace!"

"I am deeply moved by your journey and discovery of papa Lionel. Having worked with my foster child these past six years, I have become educated on that hunger you wrote about. I was struck by the truth of our biological roots and the need for connections. Carry on this beautiful reunion and the many Graces that emanate."

"Thanks for sharing your story. You're an incredible writer and your father was an amazing man."

"Wow and wow again. I'm so glad you shared as it is very beautiful and very sad. I'm practically breathless after reading your story of your heroic father. Your father is exceedingly handsome and his demeanor and pose in his photo reminds me of Edward R. Murrow."

"What a great story. I am so incredibly happy for you. I know from a recent experience, what deep emotions come when one connects with his or her birth family. Last year, through Ancestry and serendipity, I connected with a cousin, 60 years after my aunt gave her up for adoption. The emotion I felt when I met and embraced her came nowhere near her emotion in finally finding her birth family. Now for you to find your talented, handsome, romantic, adventurous, courageous father! What anyone would give to know their own unique story. I am thrilled for you. Do you wonder what your life would have been like if you had found Lionel Durand earlier?"

"Fascinating. So glad to read your reflection that discovering Lionel is a sudden life-changing blessing for which you are deeply grateful. Indeed!"

"As a member of the Haitian Diaspora, I feel so admiring and proud of your Haitian father, Lionel Durand, such an outstanding man. I am hungry for stories like that!"

"Major congratulations to John Suggs for his excellent DNA detective work. And what a relief to you to finally know your dad after so many years! You and your dad are so entwined, blessed, and fortunate to be reconnected."

"I'm so excited that you found your biological dad. How do you feel about that? I just found out my father was not my biological father. On some level, I think I knew that. My mother never told me she used a sperm donor. Your father sounds like a remarkably interesting man, and it is sad that his life ended so young. My biological father died in his early 50s; he invented cardiac equipment. I guess that explains my interest in health. It sounds like you have a warm and welcoming Haitian family."

"Wow that is a beautiful communication; you must have been inspired by Lionel's spirit! So powerful and so true. You continued down the path to its conclusion. You honored Lionel, your father, and Barbara, your half-sister, throughout. You have honored your blood, and they honor you. God bless you all, my brother. God has blessed you all!"

Appendix 3

Haiti and the Unjust Enrichment Claim

The two main criminals are France and the United States. To become minimally civilized we should say we carried out and benefited from vicious crimes. A large part of the wealth of France comes from the crimes we committed against Haiti, and the United States gained as well. Therefore, we are going to pay reparations to the Haitian people. Then you will see the beginning of civilization.
—Noam Chomsky

Haiti is an amazing country. Even though the people there have so little, their attitudes resonate a crazy amount of love and joy. It is truly inspiring to see that. My love for the country starts with them.
—Noah Munck

Haiti, Haiti, the further I am from you, the less I breathe. Haiti, I love you, and I will love you always. Always.
—Jean-Bertrand Aristide

My paternal ancestors were brought to Haiti as slaves from the west coast of Africa. Christopher Columbus arrived at the northwestern tip of what is now Haiti in 1492, naming the island Hispaniola. Indigenous people, the Tainos, were its earliest inhabitants, traveling by canoes from Central and South America; they had arrived there about 4,500 years ago. They were fishermen and farmers cultivating vegetables such as yams, sweet potatoes, and cassavas. There were close to one million Tainos. Columbus wrote that they "were very well built, with handsome bodies and very good faces . . . did not carry arms or know of them." Defenseless, the Indigenous were forced into slavery and made to mine for gold. Many died from slavery, violent treatment, and European diseases such as measles and smallpox. When, in the 1550s, Spain turned its attention to Mexico and Peru, which were rich in gold, French pirates took over Hispaniola, and some French started settling there and farming the land. Spain agreed to give the western third of Hispaniola to the French. In 1697, today's Haiti became the French colony of Saint-Domingue (Treaty of Rijswijk).

The French used slaves to work their "cash crops": sugar, coffee, rum, indigo—blue dyes were once rare—and cotton. In the 1700s, on the bent backs of African slaves, Saint-Domingue emerged as the richest colony in the world. Picture with empathy the slaves working with machetes, shirtless in the unbearable heat, on a sugarcane plantation, being cut by the leaves, with perspiration burning these constant small flesh wounds, and nasty ants biting them, being whipped or killed if not producing. Slaves lasted an average of three years before dying; the slave market was booming. One of the masters touted the effectiveness of slow punishments such as 25 lashes of the whip in 15 minutes as being most "impressive." Slaves suffered amputation, hot pepper being rubbed in wounds, and being hung and left to die. How could commerce include such a devaluing of human life?

Our basic instinct, our soul's desire, is to want freedom. Some slaves, called maroons, managed to escape to the mountains and conduct night raids, burning and killing on the plantations. Their leader, François Mackandal, was captured and burned at the stake. "By 1789, enslaved people outnumbered free people by almost ten to one in the colony. Out of a population of 556,000, there were about 32,000 White Europeans and 28,000 free people of mixed ancestry. The other five hundred thousand on Saint-Domingue were enslaved people of African descent." (*Haiti, Enchantment of the World*, Liz Sonneborn, 2019) From 1697 to 1804, eight hundred thousand slaves were transported to Saint-Domingue.

On August 26, 1789, the National Assembly of France approved the Declaration of the Rights of Man, a human rights document, yet the rights contained in the document were only applied to White men and did not revoke the plague of slavery. Sending a petition in 1791 to France for granting full citizenship, the mixed-race population was the first to ask for equality of rights. In reaction, the Whites angrily beat and killed mixed race people. France—to the dismay of Whites—granted them equality if they were born of two free parents.

In rebellion, the slaves would soon take up arms inspired by Voudou priest, Dutty Boukman, and priestess, Cécile Fatiman, to "listen to the voice of freedom, for the Whites thirst for our tears." On May 22, 1791, one thousand Blacks attacked 184 sugarcane plantations and many coffee farms: stabbing, killing, burning, levying violent vengeance for long-endured bodily-emotionally-ruthlessly implanted cruelty, vicious payback bred of the insufferable systematic utterly demeaning, relentless, brutal slave regime against the Blacks. Soon the one thousand grew to 20,000. Black revolt terrified France, England, and Spain. In the United States, Thomas Jefferson "recognized that the revolution had the potential to cause an upheaval against slavery in the US not

only by slaves, but by the white abolitionists as well." (Wikipedia: Haitian Revolution)

Former slave, Toussaint Louverture, giving his loyalty to
the Spanish, emerged as a leader of the fight for freedom
from the French. In 1794, France ended slavery in its colonies, and Louverture switched his allegiance back to France.
Toussaint drove the English out of the country, occupied the
Spanish section of Hispaniola (now the Dominican Republic), declaring himself governor-general for life (an unfortu-
nate precedent for coming military dictatorships in Haiti).
On November 9/10, 1799, Napoleon took complete power
in France. He was determined to restore slavery to the empire. "The revolution is over. I am the revolution." Napoleon
sent 10,000 troops to Saint-Domingue in 1802; the French
tricked Louverture into thinking they would negotiate
peace, but instead arrested Louverture, who died April 7,
1803, at age 59, in a freezing cell in Fort de Joux in the mountains of France.

The rebels "continued to fight without Louverture, un-
der the leadership of Jean-Jacques Dessalines and Henri
Christophe, and the rebel army finally defeated the French.
On January 1, 1804, Dessalines officially announced that the
French colony of Saint-Domingue was no more. It was now
the independent nation of Haiti (the first modern-day state
founded by Blacks, the first to abolish slavery). Jean-Jacques
Dessalines became Haiti's first ruler. He ordered his army to
kill all the French people still on the island, declaring himself
Jacques I, the emperor of Haiti. In 1806, they assassinated
the emperor." (*Haiti, Enchantment of the World*, p. 46) The
country, though now free, was politically divided and in economic distress.

Regrettably, in 1825 President Jean-Pierre Boyer was pressured to pay France 150,000,000 francs indemnity for their lost properties (land and slaves) in exchange for France's recognition of the new and free country of Haiti. French ships patrolled off the coast of Haiti with orders to blockade Haiti if the indemnity payment was not agreed upon.

Anthony Phillips wrote the following in 2008 while attending law school at the University of San Francisco and interning with the Institute for Justice and Democracy. (Use https://bit.ly/2MuJZnE to download a PDF of the article.) In 2002, President Aristide announced his intent "to pursue a claim against France to recover its Independence Debt. On behalf of Haiti, US attorney Ira Kurzban prepared legal actions against the French government to recover the estimated $21 billion (current money) extorted from Haiti during 1825 to 1944. The legal process was cut short following the overthrow of the elected government of President Jean Bertrand Aristide on February 29, 2004 . . . the subsequent coup government refused to pursue any legal action for restitution. . . . We find the Independence Debt, to be an unjust enrichment claim, and restitution could prove an important and effective tool to address a serious historical wrong. . . . the human cost of Haiti's independence amounted to 150,000 dead or 40% of the population, only 170,000 of the original 425,000 slaves remained healthy enough to work and contribute to the rebuilding of the economy of the new state. It took Haiti 122 years to repay its Independence Debt."

Appendix 4

Faith in Action International: Haiti

We are just now beginning to learn the extent of the devastation, but the reports and images that we have seen of collapsed hospitals, crumbled homes, and men and women carrying their injured neighbors through the streets are truly heartwrenching. Indeed, for a country and a people who are no strangers to hardship and suffering, this tragedy seems especially cruel and incomprehensible. Our thoughts and prayers are also with the many Haitian Americans around our country who do not yet know the fate of their families and loved ones back home. You will not be forsaken. You will not be forgotten in this your hour of greatest need. America stands with you. Help is arriving. Much, much more help is on the way. America's commitment to Haiti's recovery and reconstruction must endure and will endure. The losses that have been suffered in Haiti are nothing less than devastating and responding to a disaster of this magnitude requires every element of our national capacity.

—Barack Obama (responding to the catastrophic January 12, 2010, 7.0 earthquake at 4:53 p.m., 16 miles west of Port-au-Prince, which tragically took the lives of 220,000–300,000 people)

State sponsored corruption and violence are becoming more widespread. Haiti cannot recover its democracy if the United States does not speak up.

—Fritz Jean, former Prime Minister of Haiti

T he newest organizing project of Faith in Action International (FIAI), Organisation Peuple Œcuménique pour le Développement du Nord-Est (OPODNE), was formally launched in August 2014 when one hundred leaders from across Northeast Haiti gathered at a General Assembly. Catholic Bishop Max Leroy Mésidor (now Archbishop of Port-au-Prince) supported us. For over four years, FIAI leaders in Haiti have leveraged $200,000 public and private investments. OPODNE trains three hundred leaders to engage 2,500 people in community improvement activities like road building, tree-planting, cleanups, and teacher training. They operate three microlending programs and sustain seven economic development cooperatives (fishing, peanut, vegetable, chicken, bananas, peppers, and household and farm supplies).

OPODNE has established leadership teams in 12 towns and cities across the Northeast Department. Leaders gather weekly to tackle issues fundamental to the survival of their children and families. Communities are organizing their labor for basic sanitation, establishing computer training centers for youth, building roads to get their crops to market, and strengthening the cooperatives and micro lending programs to establish sources of income. Government may be broken in Haiti, but the people are not. We support and participate in grassroots organizing that enables those who are most vulnerable and exploited to build political and economic power to better their lives and communities.

Our model begins with bringing people together to reflect on their needs and purpose and share their stories. We help people build teams that solicit input from their neighbors. People prioritize the most important concerns they hear and then research and dialogue to understand who has the power to make changes. Building strong accountable relationships among themselves helps people build the power to hold public officials accountable. Taking action to bring about tangible changes in a community, and then reflecting on that action, increases people's confidence in themselves and deepens their understanding of the world. Through this cycle of action and reflection, people gain the capacity to transform their lives and their societies. People put their values into action to create a world that reflects the inherent dignity of every human being. We work with people from every faith tradition and those who are not religious but believe in the possibility of a better world.

The work we do to bring people together and imagine communities and societies in which all people can flourish is profoundly spiritual. In a world in which religion too often has been used to divide, we believe that faith and values can bring people together across differences, create community, and hold governments and corporations to a higher moral standard. Organizing makes it possible for people whose backs are against the wall to build organizations that they can use to negotiate change. Our approach offers people an opportunity to become leaders with a following. Through their participation, they share their stories, organize their neighbors, build political and economic power in their communities, and lead campaigns to change policies to better meet the needs of families. People not only get results that make their lives better, but they also come to see themselves as powerful agents of change in the world.

In a Zoom meeting in 2020, which raised over $10,000, around one hundred joined our "Organizing in Haiti in a Time of Crisis" conversation. Through its "Conspiracy to Eliminate Coronavirus Public Education Campaign," OPODNE is planting seeds of hope by distributing one thousand fruit trees to leadership teams in towns across the

Northeast Department. One hundred trees in each town means one thousand families will have something more to eat. Some trees are already bearing fruit enabling the people of Capotille to make jam. A generous donation by the St. Barnabas Episcopal Nursery in Terrier Rouge makes this possible. Director, Fr. Esperance Jabnel, said, "Unlike other organizations that sell these trees, OPODNE kept its word and did exactly as promised and delivered them to the community."

OPODNE is pleased to report how the funds raised through our virtual conference were used. Under the leadership of Executive Director, Florcie Tyrell, and the town of Phaeton's leader, Dr. Clonel Louis, OPODNE purchased spot announcements and did public education interviews on all local radio stations reaching over three hundred thousand people (cost: $1373); passed out 5700 educational fliers, posted banners, and did megaphone announcements at public markets (cost: $561); formed teams in 13 communities that trained six hundred leaders to check on families and share information to prevent spread of the virus (cost: $2129); distributed face masks, gloves, disinfectant, and washing stations directly benefiting 35,000 people in local communities ($5578); and gathered for prayer, assessment, and reflection to design a second phase to combat the virus. These efforts are making a difference. The Northeast Department reports the lowest positive rate of infection in the country.

****

There is a word in South Africa—ubuntu—(used by the Bantu people across Africa) that describes Nelson Mandela's greatest gift: his recognition that we are all bound together in ways that can be invisible to the eye; that there is a oneness to

humanity; that we achieve ourselves by sharing ourselves with others and caring for those around us.
—Barack Obama, Johannesburg 2018 Nelson Mandela annual lecture

On January 14, 2021, John Baumann, François Pierre Louis, Ron Snyder, Maria Revelles, Gordon Whitman, and others from FIAI Haiti warmly welcomed 38 of us to a stimulating and hopeful Zoom conversation focused on a concept paper "A Way Forward in Haiti: A strategy for expanding faith-based grassroots organizing in Haiti and the Diaspora."

Here are some highlights of this plan to expand a successful model of grassroots organizing in Haiti and organizing US diaspora faith communities and leaders (including non-religious) to advance the broader effort to restore Haitian democracy and reorient its economy to the needs of its people. With a new administration in Washington, DC, and Haitian elections on the horizon, there is an opportunity to reset the relationship between the US and Haiti, and put Haiti on a path to a sustainable democracy and healthy economic development. In an interconnected world, few countries are as dependent on each other as Haiti is on the US. More than 38 percent of Haiti's GDP comes from remittances, mostly from Haitian Americans. Foreign assistance makes up a majority of Haiti's budget.

There are three areas of work that Faith in Action International and our Haitian affiliate, OPODNE, see as crucial contributions to the broader effort to put Haiti on a path toward workable democracy and development: (1) deepening and broadening the base of grassroots organizing in Haiti; (2) building a stronger base of Haitian-Americans organized around critical issues facing Haitians living in the US and shifting US policy toward Haiti; and (3) lifting up the voice

of Haitian and American religious leaders and faith communities in support of democracy, human rights, and commu-
nity-led development in Haiti. The purpose of the activities
described is to improve life for people with the least resources in Haiti. Success would mean that small-scale agri-
culture, which accounts for 40 percent of employment in
Haiti, would be strengthened through access to financing
and domestic markets. Families would have more income,
and the country could meet more of its food needs through
domestic production. Haiti would invest more public resources in health and education, local municipalities would
have resources and support to meet basic needs and under-
take community planning and development, and families
would gain access to electricity, water, better roads, and
other infrastructure.

OPODNE, led by Florcie Tyrell, has built grassroots organizing teams in 12 municipalities across the Northeast
Department (population 358,277). Leaders gather weekly to
listen to their neighbors' concerns, meet with local officials
and non-government organizations (NGOs), and develop
plans to address issues fundamental to the survival of their
children and families. With the economy and political system in collapse in Haiti, much of OPODNE's work has focused on building agricultural and fishing co-ops to gener-
ate income in extremely poor rural and small-town communities. Communities have organized their labor for basic
sanitation, established computer-training centers for youth,
and built roads to get their crops to market. Where possible,
the organization has worked to hold local governments accountable.

OPODNE's experience in the Northeast has shown that
with limited resources and a simple organizing model (focused on leadership development, team building, listening

campaigns to solicit public input, and research meetings with elected officials), it is possible to develop and sustain teams of volunteer leaders in municipalities under challenging circumstances. Local teams are vehicles for productive economic cooperatives that supplement people's incomes as well as participation in local decision-making. They build on one of the strengths of Haiti's constitution, which provides local structures for people to participate in planning.

OPODNE recently completed anti-corruption training for all the members of its 12 teams across the Northeast. When there are municipal and legislative elections, the teams that OPODNE has built will help increase voter participation. They also will help assure that resources made available to local governments are directed to community needs. And as they did during the pandemic, they will make communities more resilient to climate-related disasters. OPODNE is currently raising resources to expand its organizing into the North (pop. 970,495) and into the Northwest (pop. 662,777) departments, which would help the organization reach more than two million people (20% of the population of Haiti).

****

More than one million people of Haitian descent live in the US, including 55,000 Haitians who have temporary protected status (TPS) until October 4, 2021. This protection is afforded to nationals from some countries affected by armed conflict or natural disasters, allowing them to live and work in the US for limited times. President Biden will also have to decide whether to reinstate the Haitian Family Reunification Program, allowing people to bring family from Haiti to the US. In addition to having a stake in critical domestic policy decisions in the US, Haitians have a long history of working with members of the Congressional Black Caucus to push the US government to stand with the Haitian people. The Haitian community in the US is concentrated on the East Coast, with large population centers in South Florida (308,605), New York City/Newark area (222,193), and metro Boston (65,658). These are areas where Faith in Action has member affiliates with a history of engaging with the Haitian community. In 2020, Faith in Action International and OPODNE began building greater support among Haitian-Americans for grassroots organizing in Haiti.

Appendix 5

A Conversation with Dr. François Pierre-Louis Jr.

Never give up on hope. Most of the greatest achievements of humanity were accomplished by tired, discouraged people who never gave up on hope. Anything is possible . . . if you truly believe.
—Timothy Pina, *Hearts for Haiti: Book of Poetry & Inspiration*

Life can only be understood backwards, but it must be lived forwards.
—Søren Kierkegaard

At an early December 2020 Zoom meeting of Faith in Action International, in a breakout room for Haiti, I met the distinguished Dr. François Pierre-Louis Jr., who is a professor of political science at Queens College, City University of New York. I decided to reach out to him for an interview about organizing in Haiti. He graciously responded: "If it is Father John Baumann that sends you my way, you know the answer will always be yes. I am rushing to grade finals before Christmas. Let's schedule a time to talk about the project in early January."

François has published several articles in Haitian and Caribbean journals. François's research interests include immigration, transnationalism, and Haitian politics. He has experience as a community organizer in Haiti and the US,

served in the private cabinet of President Jean Bertrand
Aristide in 1991, and as an advisor to Prime Minister
Jacques-Édouard Alexis in 2007–2008. He speaks saga-
ciously based on his heart-breaking, as well as uplifting, experience, sharpened by scholarly study. We do well to listen.
Dr. Pierre-Louis, 60, grew up in Haiti until 14 years of age,
and then in Queens, New York. Haiti has suffered through
dictators and contested elections for decades. He lamented
that François Duvalier horrifically killed all four of his
mother's brothers and many of his male cousins because one
of his uncles had openly opposed the dictator and his cruel
regime.

He is the author of *Haitians in New York City: Transnationalism and Hometown Associations*. His articles have appeared in *US Catholics, Wadabagei, Journal of Haitian Studies, Education and Urban Society*, and *Journal of Black Studies*. Prof. Pierre-Louis coordinated the Chancellor Initiative
to help rebuild higher education in Haiti after the 2010
earthquake. He was able to extend higher education to locations outside of Port-au-Prince.

On a September 28, 2015 YouTube on GCTV with Bill
Miller, Dr. François talks about Haiti and the tragic consequences of its January 12, 2010, 7.8 earthquake when 85% of
Port-au-Prince's buildings were destroyed. François, who
was in Haiti at the time, talked about the feeling of power-
lessness ("a horrible memory") as well as noting the resiliency of the people to help each other out despite a lack of
resources. Many citizens, including François, distributed
food and water. Dr. François talked about hopes for govern-
ing Haiti as a democracy, with a decentralization where the
people can use financial aid in their own communities. So
much of the aid to Haiti is given to experts who devise plans
which are never carried out due to a lack of infrastructure

and government corruption. Some from the Haitian Diaspora, independent of the state, are raising money and returning to their hometowns to organize and make more resources such as hunger relief and education available.

****

On January 5, 2021, I conversed by telephone with François, who was cordial and generous with his time.

MZC: Hello, François. So appreciative you would take the time to speak about Haiti, your life, and your work with our mutual friend, John Baumann, in Haiti through the organization OPODNE (see Appendix 4). How are you doing? Are you still teaching?

FP-L: It is a pleasure talking with you. I read your fascinating *Haitian Times* article. I hope you are doing all right in Los Angeles where we see COVID-19 is raging. We have had a tough time in my family. I lost my mother to COVID-19 in May 2020, and my brother was six months in a coma. So, I know the virus is no joke. Life goes on. I continue teaching college online using Blackboard.

MZC: I am so sorry for your great loss, François. May your mother enjoy Eternal Life. Glad your brother was able to survive. Hope you all take good care. Best wishes and blessings.

What was your childhood like and how was it that you came to live in New York City?

FP-L: Thanks. You as well. Let me tell you about my early years. I was born in Cap-Haïtien in 1960. I stayed in Haiti until I was 14, when I joined my family in New York in 1974. Haiti, during my growing-up years, was the best time of my life. I did not suffer from the lack of basic needs. My father

first came to NY in 1965. I was living with my mother in
Port-au-Prince, later moving to Northeast Haiti. My
mother's sister and family lived there. My mother's aunt was
associated with a butcher's market, so when it came to food,
we never had any issues. I did not see myself as poor. It was
really nice growing up in Haiti, a country with beautiful nature, though now it has suffered deterioration with so much
deforestation, erosion of soil, lack of infrastructure and
leadership, and poverty. It is not as lovely as when I was
growing up. I went to a Christian Brothers school; some
classmates were the sons of lawyers, businessmen, and professors. One classmate's father was the commanding officer
of the town. I realized there was a privileged class in Haiti.
Then I moved back to Cap-Haïtien, and the first year I went
to high school, also a school for many privileged children.
My godmother's husband was the chief judge in Cap-Haïtien. I had to take a test to get into the school, so I was happy
I passed. After my first year, I came to the US.

MZC: Where did you live and go to school in the US? What
was your family and school life like?

FP-L: Both my mother and father were already in New York.
My dad was living in Brooklyn and from there we came to
Queens. I discovered my dad was divorced from my mother.
Two of us lived with Mom, and two of us lived with Dad. We
were able to visit each weekend, and I was able to spend time
with my mother. After Jamaica High School, I went to college, Queens College. My dad bought a house in Queens. In
high school, I knew there was discrimination, but my teachers welcomed me, were interested in me, and took me on
trips such as to Washington, DC. In the summer I read so
many good books. I got into Tolstoy, *Anna Karenina* and
War and Peace. I was 17. A social science teacher gave me
the classic political novel, *All the King's Men* by Robert Penn
Warren. I got accepted to some colleges, but my father

worried that something might happen to me, so he did not want me to go far away. I went to Queens College which had a lot of Haitian students who had a similar history.

MZC: How did you get into politics and organizing? What did you learn as a young man about Haiti, your birthplace?

FP-L: I got to meet many people and started my political education as well. When I lived in Haiti, I did not know the history of my father and mother. No one told us. I learned that all four of my mother's brothers were killed by Duvalier. My mother suffered a lot. I met political exiles from Haiti and started interacting with students from Haiti who were activists. I was encouraged to get involved. I thought I could someday go back to Haiti to help after Duvalier. My father listened to the Opposition Radio in New York. I started to understand what was happening in Haiti and joined a student group on campus. Eventually I joined a Haitian political party. I quit school in 1980 and spent more time with Haitian refugees. There was a church where I taught Haitians ESL in the evening. I became more engaged. I started to protest along with several classmates. We met with political leaders who were exiled by Duvalier. My purpose was to help create a more just society in Haiti.

MZC: How did you meet John Baumann?

FP-L: I was organizing in Brooklyn in the 1980s. Herbert White, who was affiliated with Saul Alinsky and John Baumann's organization PICO, gave me my first training in Florida. I left Brooklyn and did organizing in Haiti for six years, from 1986–1991. I was put in jail twice, once for four days, once for two days. I was on the death-squad's hit list. I met Aristide, then Father Aristide, who was a pastor in a slum in Port-au-Prince and very much involved in organizing. I got to know him very well. When he was elected president, I became a member of his private cabinet. The coup took place in 1991, and I moved back to the US in 1992. I reconnected with Herb White and his wife, Jessica, who organized with Herb in the Philippines. I started a project in Brooklyn with $6,000 that Jessica gave me from her organization. I met Fr. John in the summer of 1996. I remember we met in Oakland, California, and had coffee. John is such a good man. He came to New York and John said yes, he would collaborate with me. I did some trainings with PICO. John was so self-effacing; you would never know he was a priest. He doesn't talk too much. But he observes and he acts. He gives all of himself for the good of others. There were people in the network whom I also appreciated and respected such as Jose Carrasco and Ron Snyder, who is with Faith in Action to this day. These people inspired me, and I appreciated their efforts for social justice.

MZC: How did your work with Father John start out?

FP-L: I brought PICO, now named Faith in Action (FIA), to the five boroughs of New York City. In 2001, I left as the full-time director because I decided to take a position as a professor. I stayed on as a consultant in Brooklyn. I kept in contact with John. When John's organization went international in El Salvador and Rwanda, he wanted me to start organizing in Haiti. I knew Haitian politics and the dangers of being in Haiti. When the earthquake hit Haiti, I was there. I decided to help the colleges reestablish themselves. We were able to get students in rural areas greater access to education. I was spending more time in Haiti and told John I would like to start a project in Haiti. That was 2013; John obviously supported me, and I met with the bishops in Haiti who supported the idea, and we launched the OPODNE organization in 2014. John Baumann has been to Haiti and loves the people. He never complains about the hot weather. He never asks for anything. I can't believe this guy!

MZC: Do you travel to Haiti? How is the work of OPODNE going?

FP-L: I was in Haiti from 2013 to the end of 2015 as a consultant for OPODNE and doing some work for the City University of New York (CUNY) Projects in Haiti. When I came back to be a professor, I still would go to Haiti about every two months. I would go there to meet with leaders in towns, with the bishop and priests; we organized plans for OPODNE. I put together seven money-making cooperatives with the leadership. Despite the difficulties with COVID-19 and the political turmoil since 2018, they are hanging on. Sadly, it's impossible to have a fair election in Haiti because of the many gangs, fully armed individuals. People are being held hostage not only in Port-au-Prince but throughout the country. There is great difficulty in getting the people access to pure water and food. There is a food deficit in Haiti. The young people have so much talent, and they want to do something with their lives. But there is no leadership, few opportunities for work. People go to school and learn trades but have nowhere to go to use those skills. Before they might go to other Caribbean countries or the US but now all this is closed. People must go as far away as Chile and Brazil for work, to see if they can survive. We must change the way things are done in Haiti, create leadership, get rid of governmental corruption. For the most part, young people have no choice but to join the gangs and engage in the drug trade which is a major supplier to the Caribbean and America. OPODNE is doing its best to improve Haiti's culture, education, standard of living, and leadership.

MZC: What gives you your focus and strength?

FP-L: The Haitian people. And people in general. In essence people are good. I have talked about the conditions in Haiti such as the death squads, the earthquake, the lack of necessities. Yet we have survived, and I believe God is looking after us. Also giving me hope are the possibilities I have seen. Together in mutual respect we give the people the chance to meet and share together, to see who they are (as well as to see who we are), to be able to implement the skills and knowledge they have. I have seen transformation in young people who are able to go to school or get a job. A parent who gets work and is then able to send his/her children to school. You do not need much money to do it. You need to tell people the truth and that whatever they want, with support, they can put their mind and heart into it. You do not do it because you want to be famous or take advantage of any situation or person. You do it because you genuinely care for the people. It is amazing to go to Haiti and see the effective leaders who do serve others, and relatively speaking, they have nothing! I think what amazes people when they visit Haiti is that it is not so much about material goals and benefits the people want as much as fostering the relationships they have with people. The *human connection*, something we are losing in the US, losing the primary knowledge that we are first and foremost human beings, no matter what, rich or poor. At the end of the day what is the difference between you and another? In the US usually all our material needs and more are met, but we tend to lose the human touch. In Haiti you can feel the human connection strongly. I honestly do not know how Haitians have the faith to keep going with so many challenges. I ask myself sometimes: "Would I be able to survive living with so many hardships encountered daily in Haiti?" Today so many have no anchor; they do not even know where the food is coming from. Yet most do not steal or kill; they deal with it in a very decent, human way. This faith and love for the people—despite such trials and tribulation—keep me going as an activist on behalf of my beloved Haiti. Thank you and God bless you for our conversation.

MZC: Thanks to you, François, and blessings for your work and service with and from our Haitian brothers and sisters. Thanks, too, for being such an inspiration to all of us.

65785241R00146